Cambridge Elements

Elements in Chinese Economy and Governance
edited by
Luke Qi Zhang
Fudan University
Mingxing Liu
Peking University
Daniel Mattingly
Yale University

BRIBERY AS A THIRD PATH TO POWER?

Political Selection in China Beyond Performance and Patronage

Jiangnan Zhu
The University of Hong Kong

CAMBRIDGE
UNIVERSITY PRESS

CAMBRIDGE
UNIVERSITY PRESS

Shaftesbury Road, Cambridge CB2 8EA, United Kingdom

One Liberty Plaza, 20th Floor, New York, NY 10006, USA

477 Williamstown Road, Port Melbourne, VIC 3207, Australia

314–321, 3rd Floor, Plot 3, Splendor Forum, Jasola District Centre, New Delhi – 110025, India

Cambridge University Press is part of Cambridge University Press & Assessment, a department of the University of Cambridge.

We share the University's mission to contribute to society through the pursuit of education, learning and research at the highest international levels of excellence.

www.cambridge.org
Information on this title: www.cambridge.org/9781009471947

DOI: 10.1017/9781009471961

First published 2026

A catalogue record for this publication is available from the British Library

A Cataloging-in-Publication data record for this Element is available from the Library of Congress

ISBN 978-1-009-47194-7 Hardback
ISBN 978-1-009-47195-4 Paperback
ISSN 2976-5625 (online)
ISSN 2976-5617 (print)

Additional resources for this publication at www.cambridge.org/Zhu.

Bribery as a Third Path to Power?

Political Selection in China Beyond Performance and Patronage

Elements in Chinese Economy and Governance

DOI: 10.1017/9781009471961
First published online: April 2026

Jiangnan Zhu
The University of Hong Kong

Author for correspondence: Jiangnan Zhu, zhujn@hku.hk

Abstract: While bribery has been extensively studied, the dynamics of personnel corruption in the public sector, often known as "buying and selling of government offices," remain underexplored. This form of corruption involves leaders accepting or soliciting bribes from subordinates to influence recruitment, appointment, and promotion decisions, significantly impacting political selection and governance quality. This Element employs a dual perspective – corruption and elite mobility – to analyze the distribution of office-selling across the Chinese administrative matrix and its various forms and implications. Using two novel self-compiled datasets, it proposes a tripartite framework of performance, patronage, and purchase to reimagine political selection in China, highlighting the coexistence of multiple governance models: a meritocratic state prioritizing competence, a clientelist state emphasizing loyalty, and an investment state bound by money. This title is also available as Open Access on Cambridge Core.

Keywords: personnel corruption, bribery, loyalty, political selection, China

ISBNs: 9781009471947 (HB), 9781009471954 (PB), 9781009471961 (OC)
ISSNs: 2976-5625 (online), 2976-5617 (print)

Contents

1 Introduction: Why Study Buying and Selling Offices?

Although corruption permeates society, economic corruption – the abuse of political power for business opportunities and profit – often attracts the most attention, because it can directly cause distorted resource allocation, inefficient industrial policies, reduced investment, unproductive economic activities, and slow economic growth (e.g., Mauro & Driscoll 1997; Rose-Ackerman 1999). Thus, governments and scholars are inevitably more concerned with economic corruption than other forms of corruption. The Chinese authorities legally equated corruption with economic crimes at an early stage in China's reform and opening up, as corruption intensified with economic reform (Lü 2000; Gong 2002; Manion 2004; Sun 2004; Wedeman 2004; Guo 2008). Studies of corruption in China have illustrated how various forms of corruption have evolved alongside changes in economic policies over time, from speculative and profiteering activities in the 1980s to the illegal privatization of public assets in the 1990s and the widespread exploitation of land transactions in real estate development in the 2000s (Gong 2002; Wedeman 2004; Guo 2008; Ko & Weng 2012; Zhu 2012a; Wang 2013; Sun 2015; Pei 2016; Wang 2016; Chen & Kung 2019; Li & Tu 2024). Government intervention in the transitional economy is widely considered a major cause of corruption, in addition to power concentration, the design of the anticorruption system, and cultural factors (Gong 1994; Lü 2000; Manion 2004; Sun 2004; Cai 2014; Zhu 2014). Works explaining the paradoxical coexistence of rapid economic growth and high levels of corruption in China (Wedeman 2012; Zhu & Zhang 2017a; Ang 2020) also contribute to the classic debate on the relationship between corruption and economic development (e.g., Leff 1964; Méon & Sekkat 2005).

Outside the economic arena, an important but understudied type of corruption is buying and selling government offices, which can directly affect government quality and indirectly incur socioeconomic costs. This Element focuses on buying and selling offices in China. I use terms – such as "personnel corruption," "office-buying/selling," "sale of government offices," and "purchasing offices" – interchangeably, depending on the context. By investigating two original datasets, I find that this type of corruption encompasses a broader range of activities and actors and is more extensive and deeply embedded within China's Party-state hierarchy than commonly assumed.

Moreover, office-selling cases offer a new vantage point for examining elite mobility and shed fresh light on political selection in China. They draw attention to an "elephant in the room": While previous research on promotions emphasizes candidates' performance and connections, leaders may also be motivated by the opportunity to extract rents from candidates and maximize their personal wealth during political selection. Thus, a central question is to what extent the influence of money can alter the competitive dynamics of political selection suggested by prevailing explanations. My research in this Element shows that in some scenarios, monetary gains take precedence over or even override other considerations, such as a candidate's performance or loyalty, for leaders who sell public offices, such that paying for offices is more of a capital investment for potential career advancement. In other circumstances, paying for public offices represents a seemingly minor divergence from widely understood norms of political selection. For example, bribes may be used as an alternative means to strengthen connections with superiors and even cement mutual trust. However, nuanced differences remain between personal ties forged through bribery and those based on shared experiences in traditional elite politics.

Therefore, I propose the inclusion of *purchase* as a third paradigm, challenging the popular binary view of performance versus patronage (see Manion 2023 for a review and more discussion later). The key distinction between the novel purchase paradigm and the well-established patronage paradigm lies in the primary motivation of superior officials. The patronage paradigm is principally concerned with loyalty cultivation. Patronage functions as a long-term political investment, where a superior builds an interpersonal network to ensure that their agenda is faithfully executed and to secure future career protection. The currency of this paradigm is trust and allegiance, often built upon shared experiences. In contrast, the purchase paradigm is driven by the goal of rent seeking. Public office is treated as a commodity, and the superior's primary goal is financial maximization. The distinction between the two paradigms is not always clear-cut. As discussed in Section 5, some forms of office-selling can generate a distinct type of coerced loyalty, which involves a blackmailing mechanism based on mutual incrimination. This relationship differs fundamentally from the trust-based allegiance sought in traditional patronage networks. In other circumstances, a preexisting patronage network can facilitate a "purchase" transaction, as the trust and interpersonal connections established within such a network reduce the significant risks associated with an illicit activity such as buying and selling offices. The network provides the credible commitment needed to ensure that the deal is honored and vastly reduces the risk of leaks or betrayal. In this context, patronage does not compete with but rather enables purchase. Thus, the tripartite framework of performance, patronage, and purchase reimagines political selection in China, highlighting the complexity and multifaceted nature of how individuals ascend to public positions. In navigating these pathways, leaders select candidates who offer resources and qualities aligned with the leaders' political and economic aspirations – some of which are related to their leadership roles. This multitude of routes for advancement points to the coexistence (sometimes mutual reinforcement) and contestation of multiple state models based on different selection paradigms: a meritocratic state, which prioritizes competence; a clientelist state, where loyalty prevails; and an investment state, which is bound by money.

1.1 The Notion of Buying and Selling Offices

Office-selling is neither new nor unique to contemporary China but has deep historical roots across cultures and eras. In premodern Europe, offices of the state were generally either sold outright or granted as patronage by the crown (Allen 2005; Guardado 2018). For example, the British army awarded commissions (i.e., formal documents of appointment) to officers who offered the highest payment, a practice that only ended with the introduction of professional officer corps in 1871 (Allen 2005). Similarly, in imperial China, such as during the Qing dynasty, in addition to the widely known meritocratic examination system, the office purchase system (*juanna*) was preferred by wealthy individuals seeking career advancement (Zhang 2022). Although purchase has been criticized both historically and in contemporary times as inherently corrupt, ruling authorities, including emperors and other monarchs, often sanctioned the sale of official positions as a legitimate means of raising revenue from their ownership over public offices. These institutionalized transactions were not only explicitly regulated and monitored by the state but also integrated into the governance structures of the time.

In contrast, the modern sale of official positions is a form of wealth extraction whereby office sellers abuse their power to fill their pockets, making it a clear example of corruption. Office-selling occurs clandestinely in many countries and regions today, including India, Indonesia, post-Soviet Eurasia, and even some Western democracies (Wade 1985; Engvall 2015). For instance, the former Russian president Dmitry Medvedev acknowledged that public offices in Russia were effectively for sale, with the sole exceptions of the presidency, the prime ministership, and a handful of positions in their immediate orbit; all other posts were accessible to those with sufficient financial resources (Engvall 2015). In the United States, the former Illinois governor Rod Blagojevich was found guilty of trying to "auction" Barack Obama's vacated Senate seat "to the highest bidder" for financial benefits after Obama was elected US president in 2008.[1]

In this Element, I closely examine buying and selling offices in contemporary China, where it occurs primarily *within* the government, often involving a vertical corruption network of two or more government officials. Senior

[1] See https://www.nbcnews.com/id/wbna28139155.

officials (e.g., the Party chief of a local government or head of a functional department) accept or solicit bribes from their subordinates to help them (or their relatives) with personnel issues. A narrow form of this type of corruption corresponds to its direct Chinese translation *maiguan maiguan* (买官卖官), which literally means "paying for (in monetary form) and selling the positions of public officials." A typical example is that of Ma Weiling, former head of the Shanwei Municipal Police Department, who promoted nine subordinates in exchange for payments. Reporters even drew up his rate card – from HKD100,000 (approximately RMB91,500) for a district station's political commissar to USD80,000 (approximately RMB569,568) for deputy head of the urban police department. An example from the buyers' side is that of Nie Weidong, a low-level official who bought the vice-mayorship of Sanmenxia, Henan province by bribing the city's Party secretary. He boasted that the RMB1 million he paid was a steal, having set aside RMB2 million for the job.[2]

However, this Element amply shows that office-selling should be understood broadly as personnel corruption (*renshi fubai* 人事腐败) in the public sector. First, in the official discourse of the Chinese Communist Party (CCP), the concept of buying and selling offices goes beyond its direct Chinese translation to encompass a series of similar issues. For example, a search in the *People's Daily* between 2000 and 2024 reveals a cluster of terms frequently mentioned together with *maiguan maiguan*, such as *weigui yongren* (违规用人, illegal hiring), *lapiao huixuan* (拉票贿选, vote buying), and *paoguan yaoguan* (跑官要官, lobbying for office). These terms essentially denote varied forms of purchasing offices. Figure 1 illustrates the fluctuating frequencies of core terms in the conceptual family of buying and selling offices. The peaks of several terms between 2015 and 2017 overlap with the temporal summit of President Xi Jinping's corruption crackdown. "Corruption during the selection and employment of cadres" (*xuanren yongren zhongde fubai*), CCP jargon for personnel corruption, was one of the main targets in those years, along with the arrest of many mid- to high-ranking officials such as Zhou Yongkang (Zhu, Huang, & Zhang 2019; Kang & Zhu 2021; Wang & Dickson 2022; Li & Manion 2023).

Moreover, while government officials are the core actors in this type of corruption, and government positions are often its main trading focus, the offices purchased do not always carry political authority. Buying and selling posts in other public sectors, such as state-owned enterprises (SOEs) and public schools and hospitals, and even positions of village heads, is also considered this type of corruption, because the Chinese government has indistinct boundaries and the public sphere is expansionary because of the Party-state system.

[2] See www.hkcd.com/content/2016-04/08/content_994829.html.

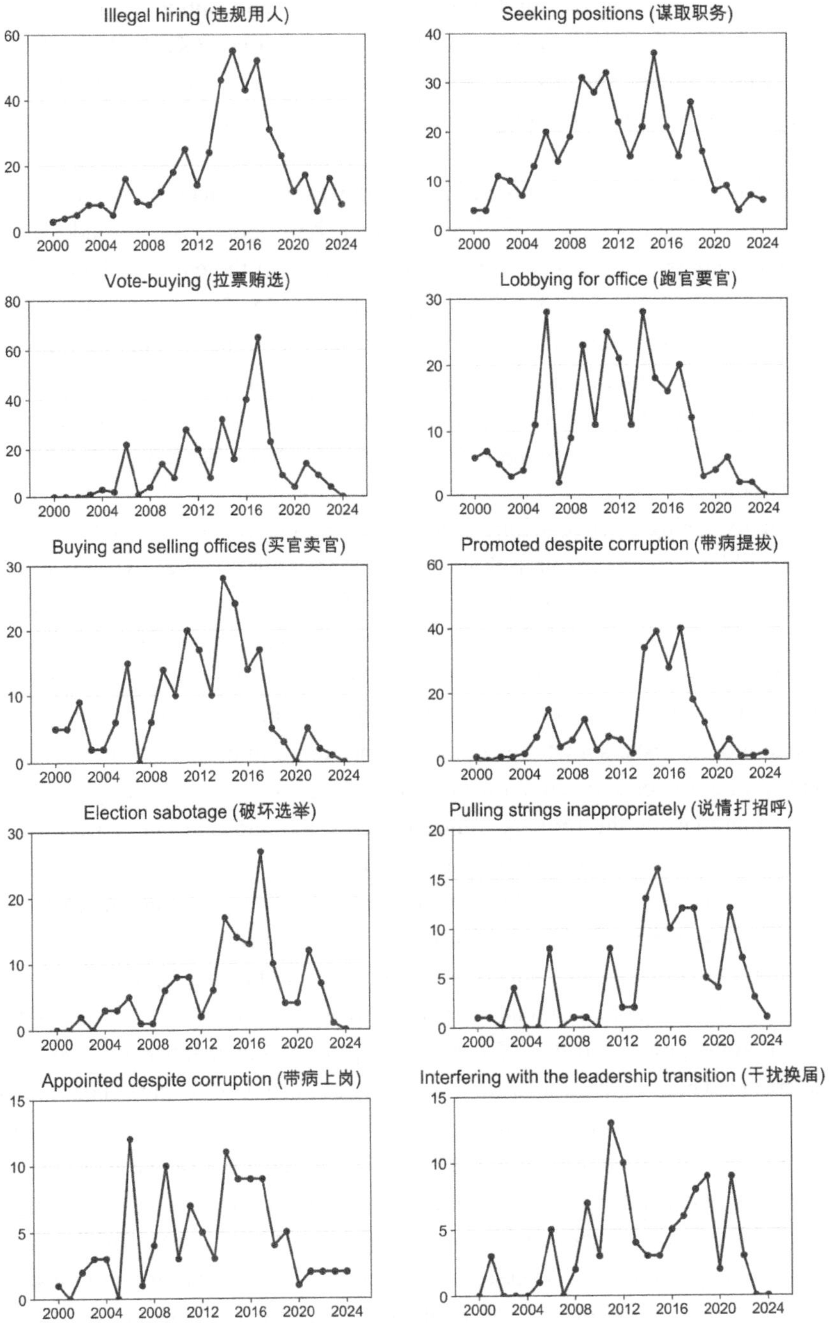

Figure 1 Top ten words most frequently appearing alongside "buying and selling offices" in the *People's Daily*, 2000–24.

Note: The y-axis shows the frequency of appearance of each term in the CCP's official mouthpiece. The fluctuations in word frequency reflect the CCP's changing attention to the issue (see Section 6).

Public organizations are funded by governments, and public employees are referred to as state functionaries in Chinese criminal law (Ko & Weng 2011). Many government officials were formerly public employees of nongovernment units. Thus, the positions bought and sold may involve any posts in the public sector.

In addition, the personnel issues involved in buying offices are not limited to officials' promotions (*tiba* 提拔 or *jinsheng* 晋升) but cover myriad career-related matters associated with public employees. At the entrance level, these matters concern recruitment, including admission to schools (as educational attainment affects one's career opportunities), and personnel assignment. Higher up the administrative ladder, personnel corruption surrounds appointment, lateral transfer (*diaodong* 调动), obtaining positive evaluations or high rankings in assessments (*pingbi* 评比), advancing to higher ranks (*jinji* 晋级), and so on.

Finally, a single office-selling case could signal entrenched personnel collusion within the government. Behind one case may exist an extensive network of multiple public employees, some sellers of offices, some acting as intermediaries, and others buyers of offices. The bribes also take various forms and come from different sources; they include office buyers' savings, bribes collected by office buyers from businesspeople, and more complicated economic and non-economic interests, sometimes delivered through a middleman. Thus, buying and selling offices and economic corruption fuel each other. Although government hierarchy is the primary venue for office-selling, the phenomenon can expand beyond government boundaries and generate more corruption. As shown later, the prices of political positions also reflect the unequal opportunities to make informal incomes through economic corruption.

Therefore, office-selling affects a core component of Chinese politics: namely, the political selection of officials – specifically, which individuals are selected to wield public power and how. The selection process and results can profoundly determine whether "those who are fit to serve" can be found (Besley 2005, p. 43), "the characteristics of public officials," and "the quality of governance" (Manion 2023, p. 1). As argued by Key (1956, p. 10), "the nature of the workings of government depends ultimately on the men who run it." Thus, selecting the right people is at least as important as supervising them, if not more so. Additionally, office-selling exposes weaknesses in the incentive system and oversight institutions that fail to hold officials accountable (Pérez-Durán 2023). Personnel corruption is thus a great concern for the Chinese authorities. Xi Jinping commented in 2014 as the general secretary of the CCP: "Corruption in personnel matters is a prominent problem; the practice of appointing officials in violation of the rules is widespread. Our system of cadre management is for show only. In some areas, the problems of bribing for votes, lobbying for office, and *maiguan maiguan* are grave" (cited in Pei 2016, p. 78).

1.2 A Dual Perspective on Personnel Corruption and a Tripartite Framework for Analyzing Political Selection

Despite the prevalence and political importance of personnel corruption in China, research on this topic is limited. To the best of my knowledge, only two English language studies to date have investigated it in great detail: The first is my case study article on a long office-selling chain in Heilongjiang province uncovered in the early 2000s (Zhu 2008), and the other is a chapter by Pei (2016) based on fifty cases of public offices for sale. Relatedly, Burns and Wang (2010) discuss how buying offices undermines the impact of civil service reform. Wang (2016) explores the buying and selling of military positions via ethnographic interviews. Sun (2004) and Manion (2023) briefly discuss possible patterns of personnel corruption relative to economic corruption. In the rare Chinese language scholarship on office-selling, Feng's (2010) participant observation research reveals how local cadres rely on monetary means to assist their promotions, and Gong and Wu (2012) confirm the prevalence of buying and selling offices in China in a large sample of cases collected from Chinese newspapers. Albeit limited in scope, these works greatly inform the current study and provide tentative conjectures for further examination.

I consider a dual perspective, combining corruption and elite mobility, to learn more *about* and *from* personnel corruption in China.

1.2.1 Corruption Perspective

This perspective, which is often presumed in prior research, including my own, views personnel corruption primarily as deviance from formal institutions violating the Party-state regulations – ultimately a problem to be corrected. This is essentially a state-centered perspective on buying and selling offices. Adopting it, we investigate the severity of this type of corruption (e.g., the levels of officials, positions, and amounts of money involved), the establishment of "money for power" transactions, the causes, particularly the institutional loopholes allowing it to occur and persist, and whether government policies have brought it under control.

1.2.2 Elite Mobility Perspective

The elite mobility perspective diverges from the corruption perspective by putting aside the illegality of personnel corruption and juxtaposing purchasing offices with other elite mobility paths argued by extant studies. This perspective may help us see the unseen, because abandoning the state approach that views informal markets as a deviation from formal institutions, as demonstrated by Reno (1995) in his research on corruption in Sierra Leone, is a necessary first step in "understand[ing] alternative methods of political organization" (Engvall 2015, p. 28). I argue that the elite mobility perspective can not only help unlock the nature of buying and selling offices but also provide novel insights into political selection in China on at least two fronts.

First, studies of political selection focus primarily on the top two officials in local jurisdictions (e.g., Party secretaries and governors of provinces, prefectures, and counties), leaving a gap in understanding of the mobility and bureaucratic appointment of the majority of cadres who work in Party and government functional departments, SOEs, and other public sectors. As He Xian, the former vice-minister of the Ministry of Human Resources and Social Security, remarked, among the 7.17 million public servants in China, nearly 80% are frontline personnel at or below the county level (He 2016). Many office buyers are these "ordinary" bureaucrats, revealing how they advance their political careers.

Second, and even more importantly, the elite mobility perspective prompts reflection on the prevailing explanations of political selection in China (e.g., Choi 2012; Shih, Adolph, & Liu 2012; Yang, Xu, & Tao 2014; Jia, Kudamatsu, & Seim 2015; Jiang 2018; Landry, Lü, & Duan 2018; Doyon & Keller 2020; Shih & Lee 2020; Chen & Hong 2021). Manion (2023) artfully categorizes this rich body of literature into the *performance paradigm* and the *patronage paradigm*. The two paradigms involve divergent assumptions about the fundamental goals of an authoritarian leader. The performance paradigm suggests that formal political selection institutions function largely as intended. Officials are promoted on the basis of comparisons of their performance, particularly in Gross Domestic Product (GDP) growth, with that of their peers. Underlying the evaluation criteria is a development-driven Party-state that values candidates' pro-growth qualities, such as competence. In contrast, under the patronage paradigm, the authoritarian leader cares the most about their political survival; therefore, informal institutions, such as personal connections and factional ties, are believed to drive decisions regarding political selection. Metrics and evaluation procedures do not effectively influence expectations about appointments. Instead, as in premodern Europe, appointments by patronage are rewards for individuals who demonstrate loyalty to a leader, awarded with the expectation that the appointees act in the interests of the patron (Allen 2005). Thus, beneath performance and patronage are two different qualities that an authoritarian leader seeks from subordinates: competence and loyalty, respectively (Egorov & Sonin 2011). Although scholars' beliefs differ on whether competence or loyalty dominates political selection and whether the two constitute a trade-off at different administrative levels, their discussion is largely constrained to the binary perspective. However, the dilemma of selecting between competent and loyal subordinates originates from the perspective of the topmost authoritarian leader, who perceives high stakes in the regime. Subnational leaders' interests may diverge from those of the central ruler. The prevalence of office-selling indicates that many leaders see political selection as an opportunity to increase personal wealth; even rulers of premodern states considered public offices to be tax farms for fundraising (Doyle 1996). Historians treat the purchase or sale of offices, patronage, and professionalism (which values performance and meritocracy) as separate mechanisms that could be used by autocratic rulers as substitutes to fulfill different needs and employed by political elites at various points in their careers (Allen 2005; Zhang 2022). I build upon the performance–patronage divide summarized by Manion (2023) and propose the inclusion of purchase as a third paradigm for understanding political selection in China.

To argue for the purchase paradigm is not to assert that bribery *is* the third path to power in China but to open a serious discussion and theorization of the role of money in political selection in China. As mentioned, numerous historical studies investigate money as both the means and ends of political appointment, especially in premodern Europe and its colonies. The influence of money, specifically campaign finance and fundraising, on elections in democracies, including their competitiveness and results, is systematically studied (e.g., Adkins & Dowdle 2002; Fouirnaies 2021; Thomsen 2023). Surprisingly, the direct interaction of money with contemporary Chinese political competition is rarely studied, as if salient corruption in China could be segmented from political selection and the entrepreneurial officials in economic reform would not also be "entrepreneurial" in the political arena.

Conventional wisdom tends to simplify the relationship of buying offices with performance and patronage, obscuring the motives for seriously considering bribery in political selection. First, selling public offices is assumed to lead to the "negative selection" (Guardado 2018, p. 972) of officials, suggesting that office-selling directly contradicts the performance paradigm. However, whether this is always the case is worth examining. Second, another tendency is to lump bribery into patronage, because bribery indicates connections between the office seller and buyer. Because of the difficulty of observing elite relationships empirically, scholars also often infer connections and factional ties from outcomes (e.g., whether the promotion of a lower-level official occurs under a superior). While reasonable, this approach potentially gives the impression that bribery is rare in the promotion context and intended merely for building clientelist ties, as well as that ties of different origins are similar. Thus, bribery is merged with patronage and eventually disappears from theorization about political selection in China.

However, China's numerous office-selling cases indicate that bribery is common and that money can directly facilitate and be a goal of political selection. Moreover, in-depth case studies show that personal ties based on money differ in many ways from those based on common experiences or ideological pursuits, including their trust-ensuring mechanisms, the resilience of cooperative relationships, and the ultimate politico-economic agenda (Pye 1981; Boucek 2009; Rithmire & Chen 2021; Zhu 2022). Therefore, overlooking bribery or conflating it with patronage may disguise important nuances of elite dynamics. Including the purchase paradigm can help explain residuals or false positives unexplained by the two other paradigms, especially at subnational levels.

1.2.3 Tripartite Framework for Reimagining Political Selection

I use a tripartite framework to juxtapose the three paradigms and stimulate the theoretical reimagining of political selection. Imagine that the 3D space in Figure 2 contains all the possible career advancements of individuals, which can be mapped in accordance with different selection paradigms. Each axis represents one paradigm, and the key qualities or resources that leaders especially want candidates to supply under that paradigm are summarized in

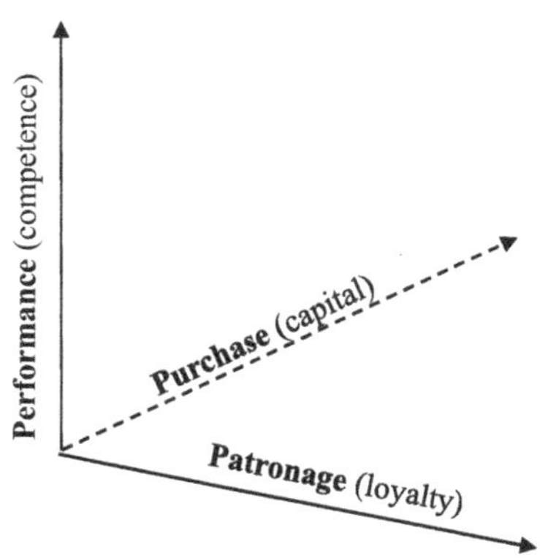

Figure 2 A tripartite framework for analyzing political selection in China.

Note: An individual's promotion outcome can be any point in the three-dimensional space, determined by the three dimensions' respective weights. Higher weights on specific dimensions denote their greater influence (e.g., as primary or secondary considerations) in influencing the promotion result.

parentheses. The levels of the paradigms are lowest at the origin and increase along their respective axes. For instance, in the performance paradigm, subordinates compete for promotion through performance, such as by delivering economic growth and other visible achievements that manifest their competence. Superior performance is believed to be associated with more opportunities for promotion. In the patronage paradigm, stronger connections are associated with higher promotion likelihood because closely connected subordinates are considered loyal followers who can help consolidate the leader's network and provide protection to the leader. In the purchase paradigm, subordinates who can invest larger amounts of capital are more likely to be selected. "Capital" here takes its pre-Smithian meaning of "money or other saleable assets that could be used as collateral" (Hodgson 2014, p. 1063), without extending to "human capital" or "social capital." I use the term "capital" to accommodate various interests transferred in buying and selling offices, such as gold, goods, and those in more complex forms. Capital is also a source of financial investment (Hodgson 2014), aligning with the purchase paradigm – investment of money in exchange for career advancement, political power, or corruption opportunities. Describing post-Soviet Eurasia, where office-selling is rampant, Engvall (2015) posits that the state becomes an investment market, and capital is invested not in businesses but to purchase government positions for higher returns. In this case, Engvall (2015) argues that money, rather than parochial ties, is the glue binding states together.

If a single paradigm dominated political selection in China, all the career advancement outcomes would fall on that axis in Figure 2. For instance, if performance were the sole criterion, all promotion results would be plotted along that axis, ordered from lowest to highest performance. If government positions were based entirely on sales, promotions would be determined solely by financial capital and fall on the purchase axis, with higher prices likely to correspond to higher ranks. The presence of office-selling indicates the potential for a purchase paradigm to unpack political selection. However, the awarding of positions in personnel corruption cases still may result from the office-selling leaders' comprehensive consideration of all three dimensions. Consequently, the advancement outcomes of individuals can be represented as points floating in 3D space, defined by the relative weights of the three components.

Therefore, in this tripartite framework, the relative weights of the three dimensions that contribute to an individual's promotion in an office-selling case shed light on the constraint boundary of different logics of the state. As Reno (1995) contends, focusing on Africa, the informal market is a contested terrain where the state and shadow state struggle for control. Buying and selling offices similarly constitutes an informal market, where formal institutions and informal governance compete to control political elites. The tension between performance and purchase, such as the choice between qualified candidates and those offering bribes, indicates the limitations of a meritocratic society in the face of financial temptations, because the performance paradigm is inferred from the formal cadre management system of the Party-state (e.g., Zuo 2015; Landry, Lü, & Duan 2018; Yan & Yuan 2020; Jia 2022). In contrast, the trade-off between patronage and purchase, such as the choice between loyal candidates and those offering bribes, can reveal whether loyalty consistently remains the primary concern of an authoritarian leader, as inferred from the political logic of authoritarian regimes (e.g., Svolik 2012). Hence, my tripartite framework can display the potential coexistence and contestation of multiple states based on different selection paradigms.

Therefore, taking a dual perspective, I connect two important aspects of Chinese politics: corruption and political selection. The five remaining sections answer the following research questions. (1) How widely is the practice of buying and selling offices distributed across the administrative matrix in China? (2) How does the process of buying and selling offices work? (3) What causes personnel corruption in the public sector? (4) When does the purchase paradigm supersede the other two, and to what extent does bribery constitute a de facto separate path for cadres to get ahead in China? (5) What are the implications of personnel corruption and how has the CCP responded to it?

1.3 Data and Methods

To answer the main research questions, I construct two datasets. Dataset A comprises data on 280 high-ranking officials at or above the vice-provincial/ministerial level who were arrested for corruption (known colloquially as "big tigers") between the end of 2012, when President Xi came into power, and the end of 2022. The dataset provides data on a wide range of variables covering demographic information, career trajectory, educational background, and corruption behavior. To construct Dataset A, I manually collect and extensively triangulate data from publicly available sources. The primary sources include the official website of the Central Commission for Discipline Inspection (CCDI), which publishes formal announcements of investigations, Party disciplinary actions, and criminal sentences. I cross-reference these with state media reports (e.g., from Xinhua or the *People's Daily*) to ensure consistency in case details and to supplement gaps in the official disclosures. These sources are further supplemented by information from semiofficial platforms, such as Baidu Baike, and selectively by international and investigative media (e.g., the BBC or the Paper). I collected as much biographical information on these officials and their political and professional credentials and as many details of their involvement in office-selling cases as possible. Dataset A contains each official's name, gender, birth year, date of arrest, administrative rank, and institutional affiliation (e.g., provincial government, central ministries, the military, or SOEs). Educational details include the graduation year, highest academic attainment, university attended, disciplinary background (e.g., engineering, law, or economics), and participation in Party school programs (coded by level and the nature of the training), enabling deep analysis of elite socialization and career formation.

Dataset A also includes structured indicators to trace corruption-related behavior, such as whether the official was involved in major collusive corruption, especially buying and selling offices, and the nature and extent of such activities. I also code how the promotions were allegedly obtained – through performance, factional networks, or financial exchange – and whether the individual acted within a broader corruption network headed by other mega tigers. In several cases, the dataset also documents specific instances of illicit advancement, locations, timelines of corrupt practices, and the amounts of money involved in bribery, based on official disclosures.

Dataset B comprises office-selling cases from China Judgment Online (CJO, *Zhongguo caipan wenshuwang* in Chinese) run by the Supreme People's Court of China (SPC). This website was launched in July 2013 to increase judicial transparency, provide guidance for lower courts on addressing specific legal issues, and enhance the consistency and quality of court rulings throughout China (Liebman et al. 2020). It rapidly expanded to include a vast collection of millions of court documents in the following years. Theoretically, according to a regulation issued by the SPC in 2016, Chinese courts at every level are responsible for uploading all of their judicial decisions to this website unless the judgments include information not suitable for being posted online, such as national secrets (Stern et al. 2021). Corruption cases can be politically sensitive. Lin (2021) estimates that around 50% of corruption cases are uploaded to the CJO website. Unsurprisingly, high-level corruption cases are rarely posted (Ma, Yu, & He 2016; Lin 2021). Only one of the 280 cases involving high-level officials in Dataset A can be found on the website. I use the keyword "professional advancement" (*zhiwu jinsheng* 职务晋升; essentially "promotion," a term frequently used in court judgments when a case involves buying offices) to search the CJO for cases categorized as "bribery and embezzlement" (*tanwu huilu zui*), denoting the crime of official corruption under Chinese criminal law. After removing repeated and irrelevant judgments, the sample comprises 460 court judgments posted online between 2013 and early 2022. These 460 cases include over 2,000 transactions, as many defendants sold multiple positions to different individuals. Each case in the dataset is manually coded for detailed contextual, procedural, and demographic variables. These include the number of positions sold, the nature and structure of the bribe (e.g., direct cash versus benefits in kind), and the type of buying and selling offices (e.g., primitive bribery or office-selling syndicates, as categorized in Section 3). Dataset B also captures geographic variation by providing the exact administrative units (i.e., province, city, and township) where the acts occurred and were adjudicated.

Moreover, Dataset B contains coded information about the major actors' bureaucratic rank, position, sector (e.g., education bureau, planning commission, or public security), and educational background, where available. It contains key event timeline information such as the date of the crime, arrest, prosecution, and sentencing, as well as sentencing rationales, including mitigating or aggravating factors (e.g., confession, restitution, or repeat offenses). The dataset also identifies intermediaries who facilitated office-selling transactions, allowing the analysis of triadic corruption networks beyond simple dyadic exchanges. Variables also help to track both the intended and actual outcomes of the transactions, for example, whether the buyer received the desired position, how many times bribes were given before promotion, and whether post-transaction gratitude or future-oriented payments occurred.

While Dataset A centers on elite-level actors at the top of China's political hierarchy, Dataset B reveals the bottom-up diffusion and everyday mechanics of purchasing offices across the township, county, and municipal levels. Most actors in Dataset B were former employees of low- to mid-level government agencies in different administrative sectors. Thus, the two datasets complement each other, enabling a systematic exploration of buying and selling offices in China's bureaucratic hierarchy.

Admittedly, neither of the two datasets is a random sample of personnel corruption cases in China. There are reasons to believe that they provide an underestimated sample (e.g., Manion 2004; Wedeman 2012; Pei 2016; Zhu & Zhang 2017b). First, corruption investigations in China can be politically motivated, and government-revealed corruption is widely believed to reflect only "the tip of the iceberg" of actual corruption. Second, court documents in CJO are selectively uploaded, persistently have missing data, and are periodically removed or inaccessible. The "missingness problem" also varies between provinces and courts at different levels, probably because of courts' different interpretations of the national rules surrounding judicial disclosure, especially regarding sensitive cases (Liebman et al. 2020, p. 185). Such problems may lead to a biased sample that does not proportionately reflect reality, and serious cases of corruption with significant negative social impacts could be missed. Thus, all frequency counts, geographical distributions, and price calculations derived from the CJO data (Dataset B) should be viewed as a conservative floor, not a ceiling, on the scale of the problem. However, the two datasets are the largest samples of relevant cases obtained to date, and their great diversity and detail reveal much about this type of corruption in China. In particular, Dataset A covers all the high-ranking officials arrested for corruption between 2012 and 2022, as the Chinese government always reports high-profile corruption investigations (Guo 2008), greatly mitigating Dataset B's poor coverage of high-level corruption cases. Court judgments generally include brief bios of the defendants and descriptions of their corrupt acts (e.g., bribes given or taken, positions bought and sold, and relevant people's testimonies). The large numbers of positions bought and sold in some office-selling syndicates also facilitate rigorous within-group comparisons. Additionally, the court judgments for Dataset B were collected before the Chinese authorities tightened public access to the CJO at the end of 2023, making the dataset even more valuable. Analyzing high- and low-level personnel corruption using two distinct datasets grounded in the most credible public information available, the overall bias of the estimates should be low. In addition to meticulously coding the two datasets to seek answers to the research questions, I conduct interviews with government insiders, such as local officials and anticorruption agents, for insiders' insights on buying and selling offices. Comparing Datasets A and B, I also draw inferences regarding court transparency in personnel corruption cases, contributing insights into courts' disclosure of politically sensitive cases in China (online Appendix A for Section 2.4).

1.4 Preview

In the next section, I use descriptive statistics of the two datasets to present an overview of personnel corruption in China, such as the government offices sold and the officials and sectors involved. I also use these findings to test observations from prior research. For instance, Pei (2016) reports that buying offices is more serious at lower administrative levels in China. Burns and Wang (2010) and Manion (2023) suggest that buying offices occurs more frequently in functional departments where bribes are readily available. To what extent do these conjectures hold after many years of politico-economic development or with enlarged samples?

Moving from breadth to depth, in Section 3, I use case studies to investigate the internal operation of buying and selling offices in detail and understand its logic beyond numbers. I categorize these cases in two dimensions: the number of positions sold by office sellers – that is, one or two sporadic sales versus multiple sales – and the forms of bribes sent by the office buyers – that is, direct monetary payment versus transfer of benefits. The two dimensions interact and yield four major types of sale of offices: primitive bribery, evolved bribery, office-selling syndicates, and oligarchical power bases. Primitive bribery is occasional, as office sellers often have better profit-making opportunities, such as economic corruption. Evolved bribery is also sporadic, but office sellers and buyers have closer personal ties, which enable the transfer of benefits. Office-selling syndicates are a commercialized form of sale of offices, resembling an investment market, that standardizes and rationalizes prices for political power. In an oligarchical power base, selling offices is a channel not only for profit-making but also for office sellers to engage in the "double defense" of political power and wealth (Zhu 2022). These four types vary in the prevalence of office-selling as the implicit rule of political selection, motivations to sell and purchase public offices, their organizational sophistication, and the importance of selling offices to an office seller's overall profit-making/power-seeking agenda.

Section 4 discusses the causes of personnel corruption. In addition to the factors discussed in prior research (e.g., Zhu 2008; Pei 2016), that is, the decentralization of cadre management since the 1990s, power concentration in the process of political selection, inadequate supervision of the main decision-makers, and huge political and economic returns from higher government positions, I argue that the rejuvenation of cadre corps (Kou & Tsai 2014; Pang, Keng, & Zhong 2018) also pressures officials to seek promotions at the earliest opportunity. Therefore, many cadres pay bribes to "jump the queue" (*chadui*).

Section 5 examines to what extent bribery represents a third path to power in China by identifying the circumstances when the purchase paradigm takes precedence in political selection. I argue that this largely depends on the alignment of resources and qualities candidates can supply with the leader's politico-economic ambitions related to their position. I find that capital supply tends to precede other factors affecting political selection when subordinates' performance or connections contribute little to the leaders' further promotion or subordinates are considered similar in competence or loyalty. Personal ties forged by bribery, such as those in oligarchical power bases, also deviate in nuanced ways from those based on common experiences. Using proxies of performance and patronage, as well as monetary payment for public offices in office-selling cases, I innovatively map office buyers' career advancements to the tripartite framework to examine their respective weights in political selection and find the purchase paradigm most salient in primitive bribery.

Section 6 discusses the politico-economic implications of personnel corruption and the central government's response to its rise. Studies suggest a negative association between office-selling and local economic development (e.g., Sun

2004; Zhu 2008; Guardado 2018). I examine this relationship by combining Dataset B with the data of Landry, Lü, and Duan (2018) and obtain similar negative results. Reviewing relevant laws and regulations, I also show that compared to the previous administrations, the Xi administration has paid significantly more attention to combating personnel corruption and bringing it under control.

2 Landscape: How Widespread Are the Offices Put Up for Sale?

I investigate the distribution patterns of office sales across the Chinese administrative matrix. I use Dataset A to study senior officials' involvement in buying and selling offices and then Dataset B to analyze the involvement of low- to mid-level government officials in such corruption. I also examine the correlation between high- and low-level office-selling. Taking the dual perspective of corruption and elite mobility, my exploration of the severity of buying and selling offices reveals how extensively it is used by Chinese cadres as a pathway to career advancement.

2.1 Senior Officials' Involvement in Buying and Selling Offices: Dataset A

As Figure 3 shows, of the 280 senior officials investigated for corruption in Dataset A, 234 (83%) are involved or suspected of involvement in buying and selling offices, indicating a fairly extensive phenomenon. Of the 234 officials, the majority (157 officials, 56%) are office sellers, followed by fifty-one (18%) who both buy and sell positions, and fifteen (5%) who are mainly office buyers. Of the forty-six officials without clear evidence of engagement in buying and selling offices (17%), some are reportedly members of the corruption networks of former (deputy) national-level officials in the sample. For instance, Ji Wenlin, Zhou Yongkang's former secretary, assisted Zhou in collecting benefits from officials and businesspeople.

Figure 4 illustrates the administrative rankings of the big tigers involved in buying and selling offices. Among the 234 perpetrators/suspects, 178 are former provincial or vice-provincial officials, far more than former ministers. This disparity arose for two reasons. First, there are more provincial than ministerial leadership positions. Second, compared with ministerial officials, provincial officials control more public posts at lower administrative levels and hold more power in different local sectors, giving them more incentives and opportunities to engage in buying and selling offices. Figure 5 also shows that most of the 234 cases involve officials in vice positions, with 170 (73%) being vice-provincial governors or Party secretaries and thirty-seven vice-ministers. One may doubt

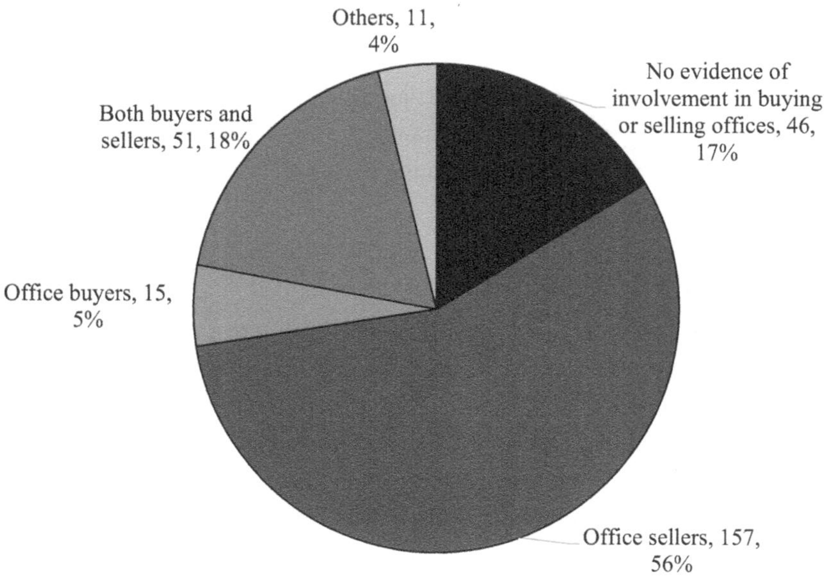

Figure 3 Big tigers' involvement in buying and selling offices.

Note: "Others" includes big tigers who are alleged in various news reports to have engaged in office-selling/buying and a few officials who allow their subordinates to indulge in buying/selling offices but do not participate directly themselves (e.g., Tong Mingqian of Hunan province).

whether the disparity results from anticorruption agencies' intentional avoidance of investigating officials in full positions. According to one interviewee in charge of Party disciplinary work in a vice-ministerial level work unit, this phenomenon arises because there are many more deputy positions than full positions in the Party-state.[3]

A closer look at the 234 officials' cases further challenges the assumption that buying and selling offices mainly occur at lower administrative levels. First, office-selling can involve or even be initiated by leaders at the national or deputy-national level. The six "mega tigers"[4] in Dataset A – namely, Zhou Yongkang, Ling Jihua, Su Rong, Xu Caihou, Guo Boxiong, and Sun Zhengcai – engaged in selling offices before reaching their highest positions and continued to do so afterward. For example, before becoming vice-chairman of the Chinese People's Political Consultative Conference, Su Rong took advantage of the convenience afforded by his positions as Party secretary of Qinghai province, Party secretary of Gansu province, vice-president of the Party School of the

[3] Interview conducted in June 2024.

[4] A name coined by Wedeman (2017) for (deputy) national-level leaders arrested for corruption.

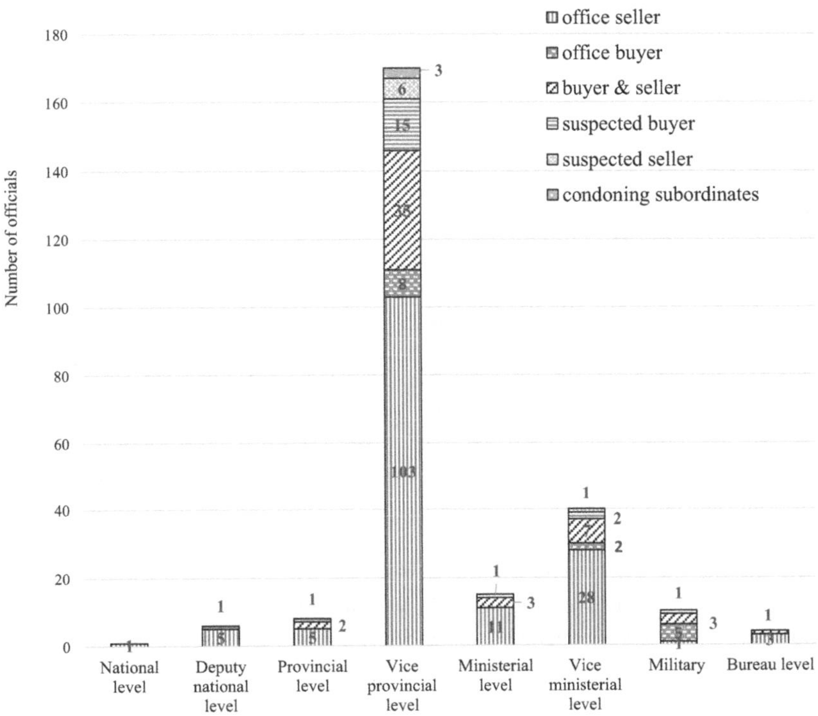

Figure 4 Administrative ranking of big tigers involved in buying and selling offices.

Note: Different colors represent different roles played by the "big tigers": "office seller" = selling offices to others; "office buyer" = buying positions from others; "buyer & seller" = selling offices to others and buying positions from superiors; "suspected buyer" = suspected by the media of paying for promotions; "suspected seller"=suspected by the media for selling offices; "condoning subordinates" = not buying/selling offices directly but allowing their subordinates to engage in such corruption.

Central Committee of the CCP, and Party secretary of Jiangxi province to assist relevant entities and individuals in matters such as business operations and job promotions. Either directly or through people closely connected to him, Su accepted property from the relevant parties worth more than RMB110 million in total.[5] Xu Caihou, former vice-chairman of the Central Military Commission, was investigated by the military procuratorate for assisting others in obtaining promotions and accepting an especially large amount of bribes, either directly or through his family members. One of his major bribers was Gu Junshan, who rose from the position of Major General to that of Lieutenant General, serving as

[5] See www.hk01.com/article/62858?utm_source=01articlecopy&utm_medium=referral.

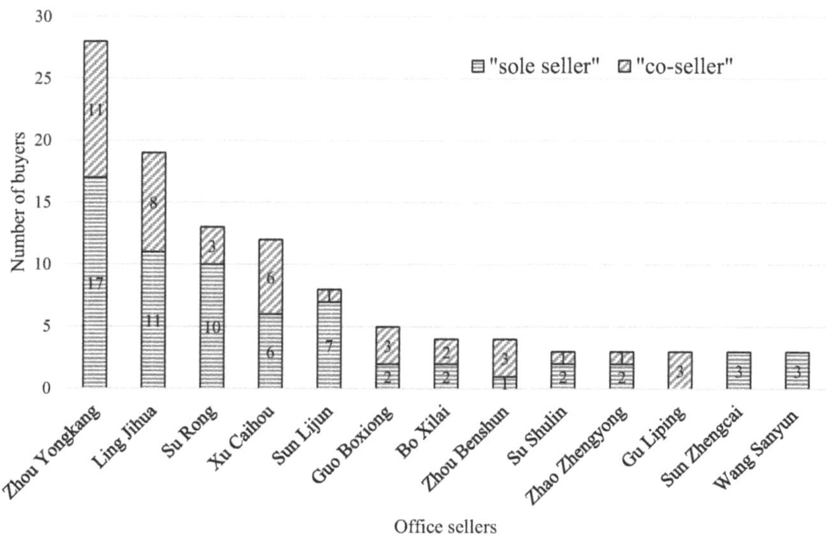

Figure 5 The most frequently solicited big tigers.

Note: "Sole seller" refers to a big tiger who was the only one bribed by an office buyer. "Co-seller" refers to a big tiger who was bribed simultaneously with other leaders by the same office buyer.

Deputy Head of the General Logistics Department of the People's Liberation Army. Reportedly, the basement of Xu's luxury residence was piled high with cash: US dollars, euros, and RMB. The seized cash turned out to weigh over one metric ton.[6] Many big tigers in Dataset A bribed these mega tigers and other big tigers for their promotions. These office buyers subsequently sold positions to their subordinates and continued doing so after moving to new posts, transmitting office sales downward and across the country. Figure 5 shows the most frequently solicited officials and the number of big tigers who bribed them. Zhou, Ling, Su, and Xu rank highest in terms of sales records, with more than one quarter of the big tigers purchasing positions from them, followed by certain ministerial/provincial leaders who took bribes and assisted with other big tigers' promotions.

Second, office buyers' rank can be as high as full or vice-provincial/ministerial level. While most perpetrators or suspects of office buyers are in the vice ranks, there are also cases such as Bai Enpei, who was already a provincial Party secretary when bribing Zhou Yongkang for further promotion. Moreover, many big tiger office buyers bribe multiple leaders to secure their promotions, giving

[6] See https://finance.ifeng.com/a/20150316/13554851_0.shtml.

birth to "sole sellers" and "co-sellers," as classified in Figure 5. For example, while Zhou Yongkang single-handedly sold positions to seventeen high-ranking officials, eleven office buyers seemed to consider it insufficient solely to bribe Zhou, despite his membership of the Standing Committee of the Politburo (PSC), China's highest decision-making body, and thus also bribed other leaders to ensure promotions. "Co-selling" forms a potential network of office sellers directly or indirectly connected through their office buyers.

Every two officials connected by a line in Figure 6 are simultaneously bribed by (or suspected of having corrupt relationships with) at least one big tiger office buyer. Wider lines mean that they are connected in this way by more

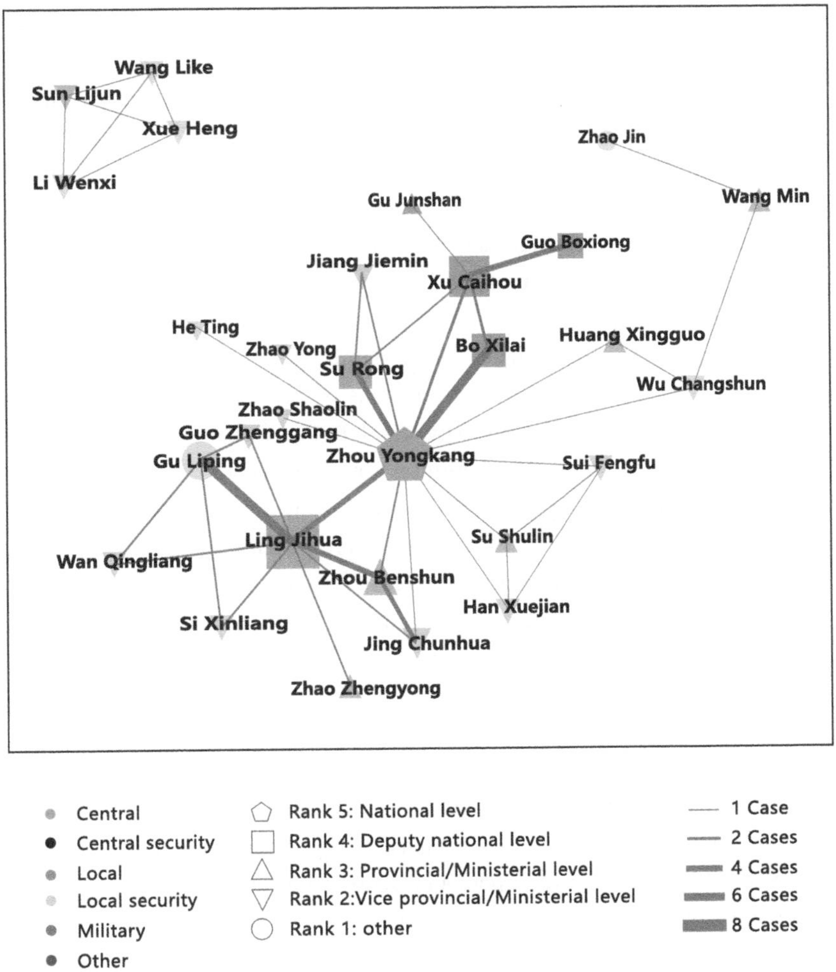

Figure 6 Office sellers' potential network formed through office buyers.

office buyers; different colors represent different sectors; and shapes with more edges represent higher administrative ranks. This network is poly-centered with intersections of shapes and colors. For instance, the dark line between Zhou Yongkang and Bo Xilai means that several officials bribed both to seek promotions, similar to Ling Jihua and Gu Liping (husband and wife), as well as Zhou Yongkang and Ling Jihua. Hence, in this network woven by office buyers, Zhou is extensively connected with leaders at the (vice-)provincial/ministerial level, and to the military, including Xu Caihou, Gu Junshan, Guo Boxiong, and local security heads. Ling's "tentacles" do not extend as widely, mainly connecting him with (vice-)provincial officials. A notably isolated seller network centers around Sun Lijun, Wang Like, Li Wenxi, and Xue Heng, a group of former high-level officials of central and local security organs. Positions bought and sold by them are largely politico-legal, such as public security and judiciary positions.

Third, money, or capital, can (help) buy a position as high as the vice-provincial or ministerial level, including provincial Party committee membership. For instance, Du Shanxue and Ren Runhou in Shanxi province and Su Hongzhang in Liaoning province received their vice-provincial governors' positions by "raising funds" from entrepreneurs to bribe leaders to vote for them. Some officials reached their highest positions at the vice-provincial or ministerial level by continuously bribing officials. Examples include Li Chuncheng of Sichuan province, Lu Ziyue of Zhejiang province, and Lu Enguang, a former vice-minister of the Ministry of Justice. The amount of money used to purchase high-level positions is formidable. For instance, Wu Changshun, head of the Tianjin Municipal Police Department, bribed other leaders with a total of RMB10 million for promotion and earned RMB84 million by selling positions. Wang Like, considering Sun Lijun having great potential for promotion in the Ministry of Public Security, bribed Sun multiple times, totaling RMB90 million, to get close to him. This was also the largest collective bribe among all the cases reported. In return, Sun treated Wang as his own man and helped Wang become vice-governor of Jiangsu province, head of the Jiangsu Provincial Public Security Department, Jiangsu Provincial Party Committee member, and finally secretary of the Jiangsu Provincial Politics and Law Committee.[7]

Finally, officials' deep engagement in buying and selling offices can also be inferred from official accusations. Usually, charges indicating that an official is involved in relatively "mild" personnel corruption use terminology like the following: "(s)he sought to obtain benefits for others and accepted bribes in the

[7] CCDI documentaries, https://v.ccdi.gov.cn/xunshilijian/index.shtml; www.12371.cn/2022/01/20/ARTI1642669016965214.shtml.

selection and appointment of officials" (在干部选拔任用方面为他人谋取利益并收受贿赂) or "abused one's position and power to illegally seek benefits for others in areas such as promotion and staff recruitment" (利用职务便利在职务晋升和职工录用等方面违规为他人谋取利益). In contrast with these relatively "mild" charges, harsher indictments are used for larger-scale, more complex, and longer-lasting corruption cases. For instance, some officials are denounced for "being engaged in (rampant) and longstanding selling of official positions" (长期大肆卖官鬻爵, e.g., Yang Keqin, Bai Xiangqun, Xue Heng); some engaged in "vote-buying and bribery in elections" (拉票贿选, e.g., Su Hongzhang); and some were described as "actively seeking or pursuing official ranks/positions through bribery" (跑官要官) and being "so obsessed with seeking official ranks (官迷心窍)" to the point of "being deceived by political charlatans" (政治骗子) or "seeking help from political brokers" (政治掮客) (e.g., Huang Xingguo, Meng Yongshan, Liu Guoqiang).[8] Officials are also charged for "seriously undermining the rules" or "distorting the orientation" of "selecting and appointing personnel," "damaging the local political ecology," and even "posing threats to political security." For example, Sun Lijun sought "to achieve personal political goals, without hesitation to use any means, manipulate power, engage in building cliques within the Party, form alliances, cultivate personal power, form interest groups, control key departments in groups, seriously damage the unity of the party and pose a serious threat to political security." Some very severe cases are characterized as "cave-in" or "landslide" corruption (*tafangshi fubai* 塌方式腐败), involving collusion by a group of high-level officials within a government unit. Several provinces in Dataset A show this tendency, such as Liaoning, Hebei, Shanxi, Jiangxi, Jiangsu, Yunnan, Inner Mongolia, and Sichuan, as indicated by their darker colors in Figure 7.

2.2 Personnel Corruption of Low- to Mid-level Officials: Dataset B

Cases in Dataset B occurred between 1993 and 2021. Court judgments indicate that nearly 400 cases continued for years before being investigated. Several cases lasted for twenty years (e.g., 1993–2013, 1998–2018), showing long corruption latency (Guo 2008; Li & Tu 2024). Strikingly, the favors sought by office buyers in Dataset B are much more diverse than those in Dataset A, which center on promotions (although bribing methods were versatile). Figure 8 displays the types of benefits sought in the 2,513 transactions extracted from

[8] The rise of political charlatans and brokers highlights the popular demand for purchasing offices. CJO has many cases involving political charlatans. Sichuan province issued a warning to local cadres to be vigilant against political scammers. https://epaper.scdaily.cn/shtml/scrb/20241221/320383.shtml.

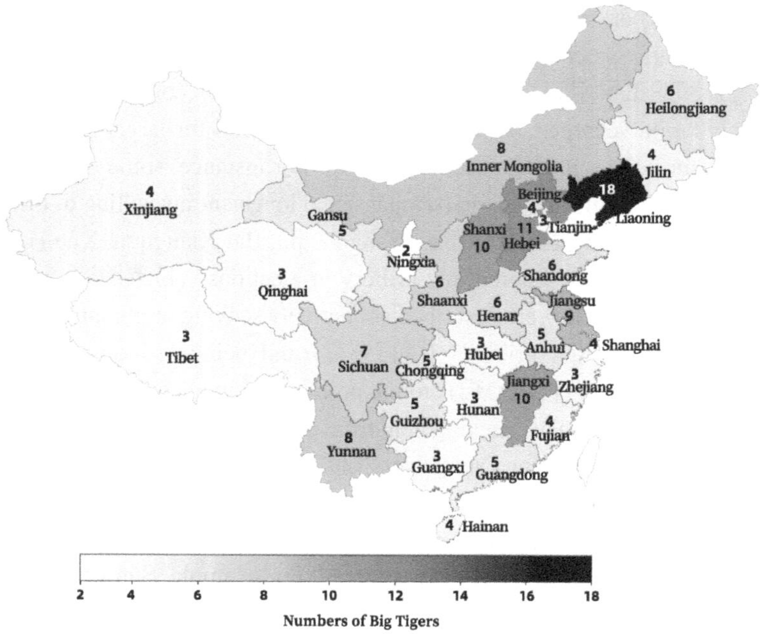

Figure 7 Geographic distribution of "big tigers" involved in buying and selling offices.

Note: Darker colors mean that more big tigers are involved in office-selling in a province.

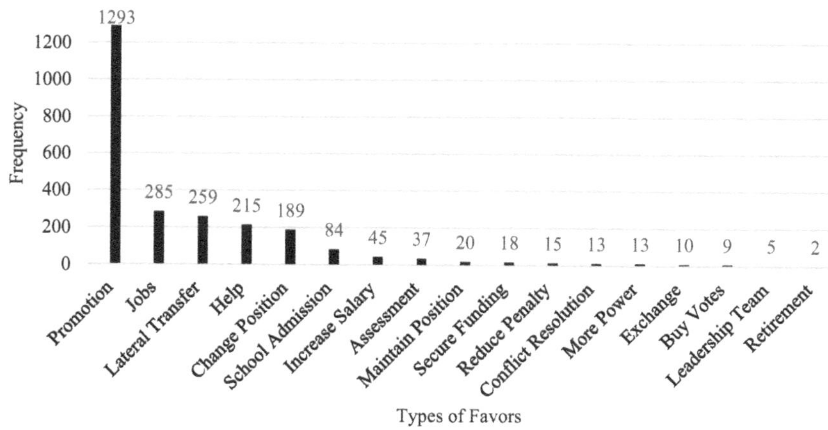

Figure 8 Personnel benefits pursued by office buyers.

the 460 court judgments in Dataset B. Promotion is still the benefit most frequently pursued, yet other favors also draw attention, demonstrating the broader substance of personnel corruption.

The second most pursued benefit, denoted "jobs" in Figure 8, concerns recruitment and job assignment at the grassroots level. Compared with those buying promotions to higher positions, office buyers of this type are less politically ambitious, mainly seeking employment in the government or public organizations, such as schools or hospitals, or a good position in the public sector after demobilization from the military. Corruption during "school admissions" is also popular. School heads or officials of the Education Bureau take bribes to help students gain entry. These cases also constitute personnel corruption because education provides credentials for career advancement and eligibility to become civil servants or public employees; sometimes they are extensions of office-selling at higher levels, as leaders take bribes for school admissions to recover the costs of purchasing offices. Personnel corruption at the grassroots level in China resembles the hidden market transactions of civil service positions in Indonesia, where people are willing to make huge investments, including buying diplomas, to "secure an earning position with stability and reasonable income opportunities" (Kristiansen & Ramli 2006, p. 208). Similar practices also occur widely in Kyrgyzstan, where individuals buy postgraduate degrees, such as *kandidat nauk* and *doctor nauk*, for specified prices to seek career advancement or leadership positions, making education one of the most corrupt sectors in the country (Liebert 2014).

Figure 8 also shows that cadres already in the public sector may bribe leaders for higher salaries, more power in their current positions, better retirement treatment, or simply to maintain their positions during personnel shuffling. Some officials pay to increase their career mobility to boost their promotion opportunities, such as seeking lateral transfers at the same rank, position changes within the original work units, and exchanges to other systems or localities (*jiaoliu*). Some lateral transfers are essentially promotions (Manion 2023). Officials also bribe superiors for better assessment results, as rankings in performance evaluations can directly affect their pay and opportunities for further promotion. Zuo (2015) documents that the method and process of cadre evaluation at the county level and above have been formalized since 2006, and leaders' career advancement is closely "pegged to assessment results" (p. 963). Although gaming the evaluation data is not easy, because it requires collusion between members of the organization department and the evaluation office one level up, local leaders, and the relevant government departments (Zuo 2015), thirty-seven individuals in Dataset B still offer bribes for this purpose.

Some officials in the dataset bribe leaders on other matters that could indirectly affect their achievements and promotions, such as securing funding for their work units, requesting that superiors appoint an easier-to-work-with leadership team, or removing disciplinary punishment records. There is also blatant bribery to buy leaders' favorable votes on personnel issues. Another high-frequency favor is "help" (*guanzhao*) (see Figure 8), which involves seeking generic assistance or preferential treatment from superiors. This kind of bribery is aimed largely at relationship-building with leaders for long-term benefits. I discuss personal tie cultivation through bribery further in Section 5.

Second, diverse public sectors/actors are involved in buying and selling offices at lower administrative levels. Figure 9 lists the top twenty domains by the counts of court judgments in Dataset B. This list partially confirms the previous conjecture that buying offices tends to occur in functional departments where bribes are readily available (Burns & Wang 2010; Manion 2023). For instance, the Urban Construction and Housing Bureau and Land Bureau have been involved in real estate corruption since the 2000s (Zhu 2012a; Chen & Kung 2019; Ang 2020). The high rank of the Public Security Bureau and the positioning of the Political–Legal Committee and court as the last two in the list seem to echo several high-level office-selling cases previously identified in the security system in Dataset A. However, also ranking high are local decision-makers, such as Party secretaries and

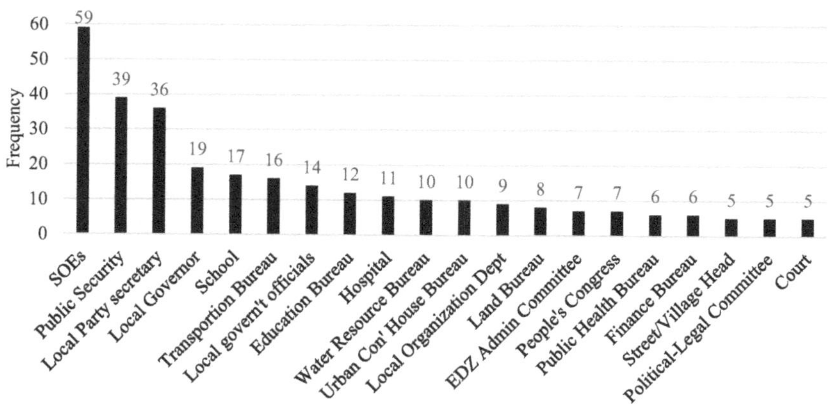

Figure 9 Top twenty sectors by counts of court judgments.

Note: EDZ denotes "economic development zone."

governors of local governments, and organization departments, which are the primary actors controlling personnel matters. More unexpected is the ranking of SOEs at the top in Figure 9, as one may expect SOEs, as business entities, to rely more on objective indicators to select leaders and have less room for corrupt manipulation. However, the frequent occurrence of personnel corruption in SOEs indicates that they, similar to their political counterparts, have inherent discretion and opacity in leadership selection.

The prices of positions also vary greatly across sectors (Table 1), which again indicates the inequality of opportunities to generate informal income across sectors (Kristiansen & Ramli 2006; Zhu & Wu 2014). For instance, SOEs rank first again, with an average payment more than ten times greater than that in the "cheapest" sector, public health. The largest bribe in Dataset B, RMB4.91 million, was paid by a subsidiary company manager of Tibet City Development Corporation to the corporation chairman for multiple promotions between 2017 and 2019. The Urban Construction and Housing Bureau and Public Security Bureau rank high in Table 1. As Burns and Wang (2010) argue, some government departments have "wet" functions that provide civil servants "with opportunities to collect rents from the public" and "recoup the sums they paid for their positions" (p. 69). The price variance in Table 1 suggests that some such functions are "wetter" than others and therefore more attractive to office buyers. List 1 shows the domains appearing both in my top twenty list and that of Burns and Wang (2010), as well as the wet functions emphasized by Burns and Wang (2010).

List 1 "Wet" functions of some of the top functional departments

Urban Construction and Housing (approvals)
Transportation (licenses)
Public Security/Political–Legal/Court (investigation and case outcomes)
Finance Bureau (tax, budgets)
Land Bureau (land use; investment approvals, zoning approvals)
Education (inspections; textbook approvals, school admissions)
Taxation (fines)
Public Health Bureau (drugs, approvals)
Local officials in general (procurement)

Note: Functional departments are listed based on their average payments in Table 1 from high to low. "Wet" functions in parentheses are identified by Burns and Wang (2010).

Table 1 Average payment per purchase in main sectors

Sector	Average payment (RMB)	Number (*n*)	Standard deviation
SOEs	261,632	217	688,485
Urban Construction and Housing Bureau	213,747	33	609,825
Transportation Bureau	193,539	38	374,942
Tobacco Bureau	157,421	19	287,778
EDZ Administration Committee	123,813	28	394,113
Public Security	121,850	250	568,077
Finance Bureau	119,897	30	296,977
Courts	96,414	9	141,877
Schools	94,172	200	543,558
Land Resources Bureau	86,554	55	259,340
Water Resources Bureau	80,535	71	300,939
Taxation Bureau	58,807	70	102,518
Hospitals	47,541	93	71,000
Education Bureau	32,433	130	122,205
Public Health	22,581	73	37,800

Note: Average payments and standard deviations are based on office-sales exchanges recorded in the court judgments. Some sectors have fewer judgments, but each judgment contains several exchanges.

2.3 Ranks and Positions of Office Sellers and Buyers at Lower Levels

Figure 9 shows the ranks and positions of office sellers at low administrative levels, focusing on the top twenty sectors. In addition to the administrative rankings, I separate officials by three types of positions: head (*zhengzhi*), deputy head (*fuzhi*), and other leaders (i.e., any leadership positions other than the top two, for example, chairman of local people's congress, member of a Party committee). Figure 10 shows that in the top twenty sectors, most office sellers have the chief position. Being the most powerful official in a jurisdiction gives them many advantages in engaging in selling offices. This contrasts with Dataset A, where vice-provincial officials are predominant. Regarding rank, most office sellers are between vice-township/section (*fuke*) and county/

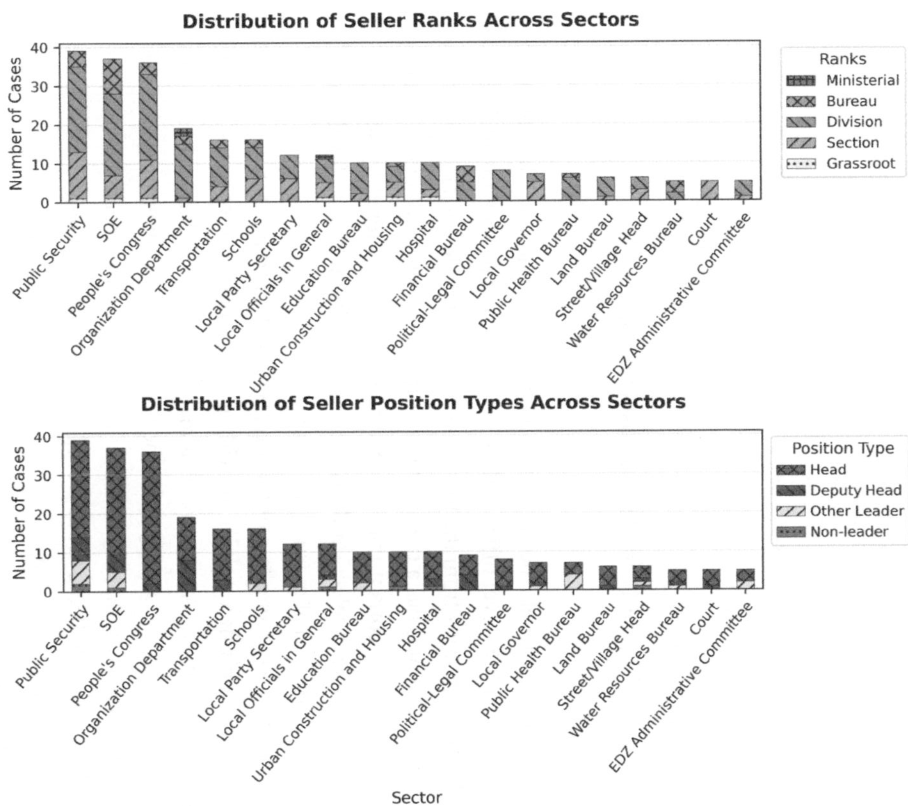

Figure 10 Ranks and positions of office sellers in the top twenty sectors.

Note: All ranking categories include both the full and deputy levels.

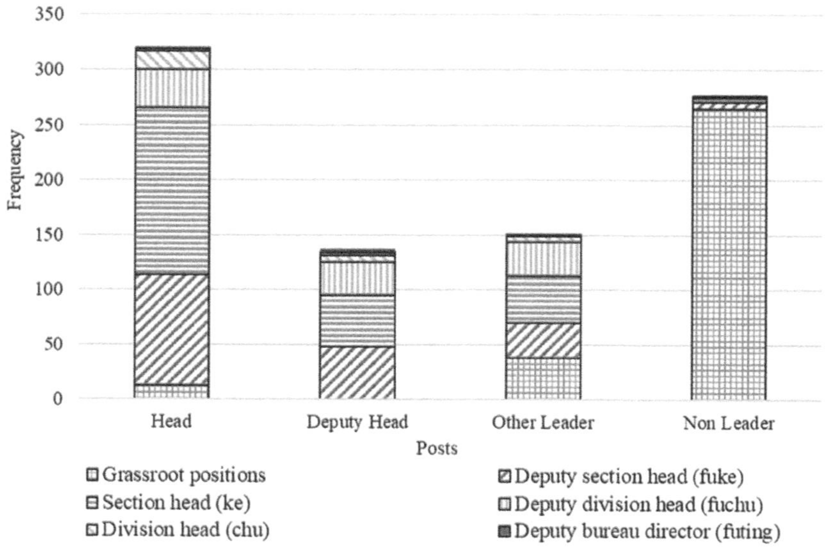

Figure 11 Ranks and positions purchased.

division (*zhengchu*) level, the most common low- to mid-level bureaucratic ranks. Thus, most low-level office sellers in the dataset are departmental heads or local Party secretaries from the township to the county level. Their power to decide personnel issues has a theoretical implication: If these officials consider money to be more important than competence or loyalty offered by subordinates, then the political selection dynamics at low administrative levels could greatly deviate from what existing studies show.

What kind of cadres tend to pay for promotions? Unfortunately, many court judgments focus on office sellers, providing less personal information on the office buyers. However, we can infer that many buyers are sellers' subordinates in the same sector and reversely infer their rankings from their pursued positions. Figure 11 shows that office buyers primarily seek "head" positions – probably because, first, being heads would make it easier for them to recover the costs of buying positions, and, second, only being a head is considered a real promotion, as power, rankings, salaries, and other benefits are tied to positions. One government insider explained, "A bureaucrat (*li*, bureaucratic clerk) becomes an official or a leader (*guan*) only after taking the chief position of a work unit because they start to hold the real power."[9] In terms of ranking, the majority of the office buyers seek *ke* or *fuke* positions, which are the lowest

[9] Interview conducted in January 2023.

ranks in the formal civil servant system. In other words, most office buyers in Dataset B originally stay at the bottom of the power hierarchy.

I also test whether higher prices are charged for higher ranks and positions by running Ordinary Least Squares (OLS) regressions. The dependent variable is the amount of money paid by office buyers for their posts in Dataset B, and the natural log (ln) value is taken to normalize the distribution. The key independent variables are the ranks and positions of the posts purchased. Ranks cover the eight levels from *fuke* (vice-sectional, set as "1") to vice-provincial level (set as "8"); and positions include non-leadership positions (set as "1"), other leadership positions (set as "2"), deputy head (set as "3"), and head (set as "4"). I also control for the sectors, provinces, and the year of office-selling cases in Models 4 and 5. The results (Table 2) show a consistently robust correlation between higher prices and higher ranks. For instance, in Model 1, an increase in rank of one level leads to nearly 45% rise in Lnprice and more than double the original money, holding everything else constant. The association between price and position is less stable across models. The prices of positions may have collinearities with rank and sector, although if considering only the average price, that of head (RMB118,246) is more than double that of a non-leadership position (RMB54,090).

2.4 Geographic Landscape of Personnel Corruption

Figure 12(a) maps the number of court judgments in each province collected in Dataset B, and Figure 12(b) is the sum of public positions bought and sold in each province. In both figures, the same cluster of five neighboring provinces, Hubei, Henan, Anhui, Shandong, and Jiangsu, shows the highest intensity of personnel corruption. They are followed by Liaoning and Sichuan provinces, which also have fairly high numbers of office-selling cases. These provinces feature "cases inside a case." For example, Shandong province has thirty-nine court judgments, which include 401 specific cases, indicating that many cases involve sales of multiple positions. This is a signal that the organized sale of offices has become an implicit rule of political selection in a locality or work unit.

Here, one may ask whether the regional distribution of cases in Figure 12 simply mirrors the differing levels of CJO transparency across regions instead of the actual levels of personnel corruption. Liebman et al. (2020) show that court transparency in China varies greatly, mainly because of local courts' different interpretations of the Supreme Court's disclosure rules. The previously discussed five neighboring provinces in Figure 12 do have relatively high overall court transparency in Wu et al. (2022). However, several corruption hotspots in Figure 12, such as Liaoning, Sichuan, and Yunnan, do not show high

Table 2 Prices for ranks and positions in Dataset B

	Dependent variables: Total amount of RMB paid				
	Model 1	**Model 2**	**Model 3**	**Model 4**	**Model 5**
Rank purchased	0.448***		0.524***	0.490***	0.235**
	(0.034)		(0.042)	(0.044)	(0.081)
Position purchased		0.171***	−0.128***	−0.154***	−0.130*
		(0.036)	(0.041)	(0.042)	(0.069)
Sector				Controlled	Controlled
Province					Controlled
Year					Controlled
Constant	9.195***	9.780***	9.347***	9.556	8.988***
	(0.089)	(0.103)	(0.101)	(0.139)	(0.358)
Observations	885	885	885	885	306
Adjusted R^2	0.161	0.024	0.169	0.210	0.359

Notes: OLS models with robust standard errors are reported. The number of observations is smaller than the sample size of Dataset B due to missing data of different variables. ***$p < 0.01$, **$p < 0.05$, *$p < 0.1$.

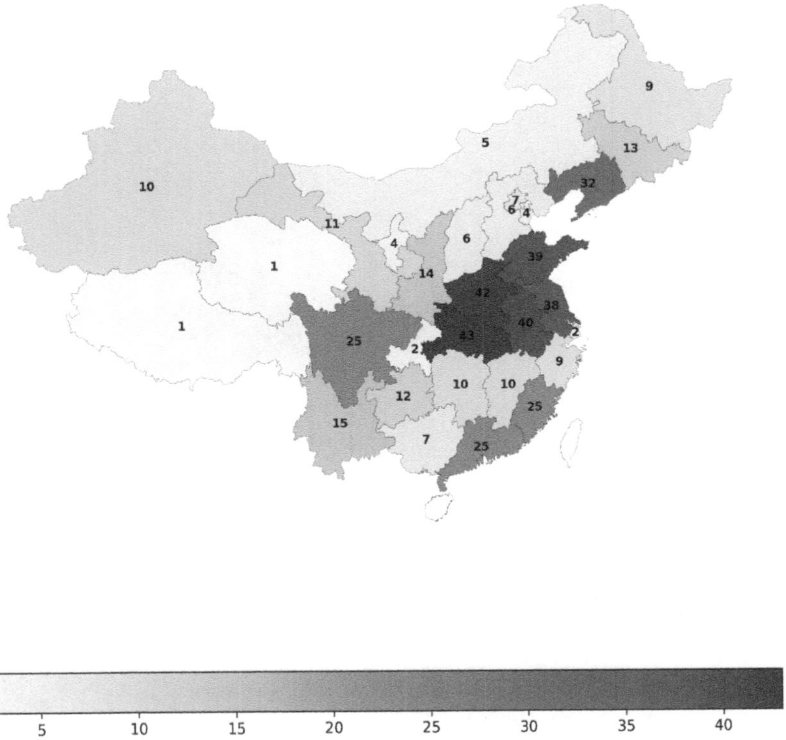

Figure 12 Geographic distribution of personnel corruption at lower administrative levels (a) Number of cases.

court transparency in Wu et al. (2022). This inconsistency dismisses the observed geographic clustering as a pure reflection of court transparency and, instead, indicates the potential impact of actual personnel corruption at local levels and reflects the fact that cases of personnel corruption – as politically sensitive criminal cases – have their own court disclosure rules and patterns, which may arise from the corruption of and crackdown on high-level officials. Hence, I further test the potential correlation between personnel corruption in Datasets A and B. Grand office-selling cases in Dataset A are investigated by the central government, reflecting both actual grand personnel corruption and central authorities' endeavors to combat such corruption (e.g., Wedeman 2012; Zhu & Zhang 2017b). The cases in Dataset B reflect both investigated local personnel corruption (which is a confounded reflection of actual local personnel corruption) and local courts' transparency. The actual personnel corruption revealed in the two datasets can be interconnected because the corruption at different administrative levels may be mutually reinforcing, forming an underlying norm of promotion in a province. If high-level officials purchased their

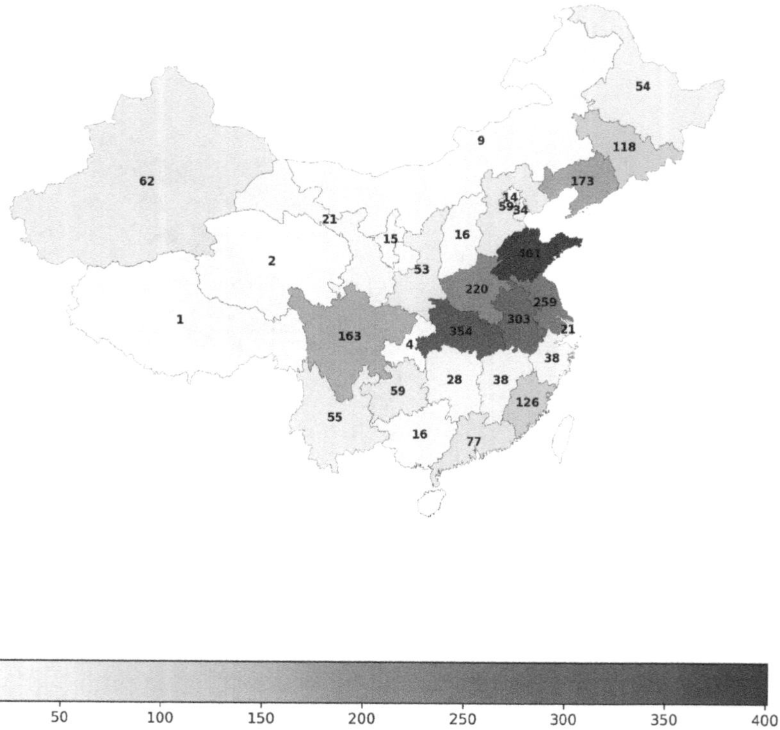

Figure 12 (b) Number of positions bought & sold.

positions from their superiors, they have greater incentives to sell positions to their subordinates to recover their costs; from below, if lower-level officials sell positions to others, they have more capital with which to bribe their superiors for promotion. Therefore, if the central government cracks down on personnel corruption of provincial-level officials, more personnel corruption of low- to mid-level officials may be uncovered in this province. The result of a simple OLS regression supports my conjecture regarding the positive correlation between grand and lower-level personnel corruption (see online Appendix A). Utilizing this correlation, I also draw some inferences about court transparency in personnel corruption cases in online Appendix A.

Geographic mapping (e.g., Figures 7 and 12) so far shows no clear correlation between the distribution of grand or low-level office-selling and either the regions or the level of local economic development. In Section 6, I use multiple measures to statistically examine the relationship between personnel corruption and the local economy. Overall, the findings in this section demonstrate that buying and selling offices are both administratively and geographically widespread in political selection in China. Its influence is wider and deeper than expected based on conventional assumptions regarding formal institutional qualities and economic corruption opportunities.

3 Typology: How Does the Sale of Offices Work?

I categorize the sale of offices by selecting one dimension from each side of a case – the seller and buyer – that is recognizable, distinctive, and broadly applicable to various forms of personnel corruption across sectors. The first dimension is the number of positions sold by an office seller: one or two positions sold sporadically or more than two positions sold over time. A greater number of positions sold indicates the greater prevalence of bribery as the implicit rule for gaining promotion under the office seller. The second dimension is the form of bribes offered by the office buyers: direct monetary payment versus transfer of benefits. In the former situation, bribes are usually given directly to the office seller and take a clear monetary form, similar to buying commodities. In the latter, bribes are more complicated, often involving hidden economic interests (e.g., business opportunities to office sellers' relatives) or nonmonetary forms (e.g., mistresses). Because of their complexity, benefit transfers tend to require more relationship building and maintenance than direct monetary payments, potentially entailing more relatives of corruption participants and leading to and reinforcing personal connections. Thus, in such cases, the paradigms of purchase and patronage intertwine. I examine personal ties based on bribes, especially their deviation from those in the traditional patronage paradigm, in Section 5.

Combining the two dimensions yields a two-by-two table of four forms of buying and selling offices: primitive bribery, evolved bribery, office-selling syndicates, and oligarchical power bases (Table 3).

3.1 Primitive Bribery

In primitive bribery, office sellers sell public posts sporadically, only once or twice. Primitive bribes also take a relatively simple form, usually direct monetary payment to the office seller in exchange for a government post or single promotion. However, this does not mean that the office sellers in these cases are less corrupt than those involved in other types of office-selling. They may also engage in more profitable economic corruption, such as taking kickbacks from construction projects or procurements.

The case of Fu Zhanwen in Dataset B exemplifies primitive office-buying. Having been the trade union president of a subsidiary company of a large local coalmine SOE for a long time, Fu sought a new position from his manager Yang, giving him a bank card loaded with RMB100,000 in early 2011. Yang

Table 3 A typology of buying and selling offices

Office sellers		Office buyers: Form of bribes	
		Direct monetary payment	**Transfer of benefits**
Number of positions sold	Sporadic positions	*Primitive bribery*: (1) Sale of offices takes a simple form (2) Can be relatively random Example: Fu Zhanwen's case, reported in Section 3.1	*Evolved bribery*: (1) Sale of offices takes a more advanced form (2) May include intermediaries (3) Can occur continuously (4) Can be a byproduct of various interest exchanges Example: The case of Wang Qiang in Maotai town
	Several positions	*Office-selling syndicates*: (1) Sale of offices is a business operation (2) Frequent, sometimes overt (3) Well-organized, for example, rationalized/standardized prices, speedy delivery of posts (4) Implicit norm of promotion Example: Office-selling chain in Heilongjiang, extensive votes-buying in Liaoning	*Oligarchical power bases*: (1) Sale of offices is integrated into complicated personal networks that combine power and wealth goals (2) Involves "double defense" of power and wealth Example: Zhou Yongkang's corruption empire, Ling Jihua's Xishan Society

Note: Some cases are not clear-cut and occur at the intersections between types.

transferred half of the money to his bank account and kept the remainder for daily expenses. A few months later, Fu was transferred by Yang to serve as head of the manufacturing department. An interesting detail of this straightforward case also sheds light on pricing in office-selling. Fu originally wanted a more senior position, but having doubts about Fu's eligibility, Yang only gave him a lateral transfer, instead of a promotion, and returned half of the money to him. This case shows that a lateral transfer is worth half of a promotion and that even under the influence of money, office buyers' competence may still be considered by office sellers. In Section 5, I discuss the relationship among the three paradigms in greater depth.

The case of Guo Zaibin, a former general manager of a Beijing SOE in land development, echoes my previous argument that office-selling is not the most lucrative "business" in which office sellers involved in primitive bribery may engage. In 2016, Guo took advantage of his position as deputy secretary of the Party committee and general manager to help promote his subordinate, who had offered him shares of a technology firm worth RMB200,000. However, this accounted for no more than 3% of Guo's total proceeds from corruption, which exceeded RMB7.6 million. Guo collected this income mainly by colluding with other companies on government projects in exchange for purchasing houses several million RMB below the market value. Selling offices was only his side business, in which he engaged opportunistically.

3.2 Evolved Bribery

Primitive bribery may escalate into evolved bribery as bribes become more sophisticated, such as taking less explicitly pecuniary forms or more indirect routes (e.g., involving intermediaries). In some evolved bribery cases, office buying results from continuous bribe-giving or is a byproduct of various interest exchanges over time. For example, an office buyer who gains a better position through bribery may subsequently assist the office seller in acts of corruption.

For example, Wang Qiang, the former mayor of Maotai town, where the famous Chinese rice liquor Maotai is produced, used his position and power to help promote another individual to deputy mayor of a town-level city. Although this case involved only one seller, one buyer, and a single promotion, the bribery occurred more subtly than a primitive bribe. The briber cultivated a close relationship with the office seller, visiting Wang repeatedly during the Spring Festival from 2013 to 2018 and sending him expensive Maotai liquor and other luxurious gifts. When Wang had a car accident, he took his car for repair and paid for vehicle maintenance fees. Over the years, these bribes totaled RMB421,318 – a relatively large sum for a position at the deputy section (*fuke*) level, whose average price in Dataset B was about RMB50,695. However, as officials in Maotai town can influence the production and licensing of Maotai liquor, a tool commonly used in China to build political connections (e.g., Lin et al. 2025), the value of the position obtained was significantly higher than that of an ordinary deputy section post.

The use of intermediaries often signals evolved bribery. Intermediaries help the main parties to distance themselves from corruption and avoid detection (Hasker & Okten 2008). For example, intermediaries may pass bribes from the office buyer to the office seller and even keep some as "commission." Sometimes intermediaries are businessmen who (un)willingly paid bribes on behalf of the office buyer to the office seller. As they are trusted by both the office buyer and seller, intermediaries can also act as guarantors to help establish, maintain, and consolidate relationships between the two sides. For example, Wang Xinping, a deputy director of the Second Discipline Inspection and Supervision Office of the Xiangtan Municipal Commission for Discipline Inspection (CDI), relied on Hu as an intermediary to introduce him to Li, a former deputy secretary of Hunan Provincial CDI in charge of personnel matters. Hu accompanied Wang on multiple visits to Li. During their initial meeting, Wang gave Li an envelope containing RMB5,000 in cash. This was followed by several more cash payoffs at various locations, including restaurants, hotels, and fishing trips, and in the presence of other people, such as Li's friend and mistress and her friend, indicating a growing trust between the parties. This contrasts with primitive bribery, which provides little opportunity for the two parties in office-selling to associate with other people.

Wang Gengdong's case illuminates other defining features of evolved bribery. Wang became the director of the Qingyuan City Land Reserve Bureau in 2008, a mid-rank (*zhengchu* division head level) leadership position. Within a year, he was able to influence the decisions of Party committee meetings and promote Feng to the position of deputy researcher (*fuchu* level). In return, Feng first bought Wang a car worth RMB156,800, then gave him HKD500,000.[10] Thus, in this case, bribes were sent after the promotion. Procurators I interviewed explained that *post hoc* payments are technically more difficult to investigate and identify as bribes that influence personnel decisions. This is partly why some subordinates pay off their superiors after promotion.[11] At that point, Wang and Feng began to collaborate. Wang exchanged the original

---

[10] According to my interviewees, bribers send foreign currencies (e.g., US dollars, HK dollars) to impress bribees accustomed to seeing RMB; to maintain the value of bribes against the depreciation of RMB; for easy storage of a large sum of money physically (e.g., 1 USD is worth nearly RMB 8) given that bribes are often transacted in cash; and for the convenience of usage overseas.

[11] Interview conducted in February 2024.

HKD500,000 for RMB400,000 and let Feng invest the money. In the following years, Feng shared monthly dividends totaling RMB228,000 with Wang and returned the principal RMB400,000 to Wang in 2017. Feng also handled several deals for Wang as an intermediary after being promoted by Wang. For instance, after Wang was transferred to the Municipal Bureau of Culture, Radio and Television, Feng utilized Wang's former influence in the land reserve and brokered a joint real estate development project for a businessman, who gave Wang about HKD500,000. These examples demonstrated the increasingly intertwined interests of, and probably trust between, Wang and Feng, in contrast with primitive bribery and office-selling syndicates (to be discussed next); bribers in the latter two forms are more like "customers" of the bribees (Schelling 1971).

3.3 Office-Selling Syndicates

While the sale of offices is sporadic in the context of primitive bribery, office-selling syndicates resemble illegal businesses in organized crime. I borrow the term "syndicate" from criminology studies. While "organized crime" is an ill-defined term, scholars generally agree on four primary elements: "a continuing organization, an organization that operates rationally for profit, the use of force or threats, and the need for corruption to maintain immunity from law enforcement" (Albanese 2000, p. 411). Office-selling syndicates meet these criteria. It is operated as an ongoing criminal enterprise, with the higher-ranking office seller frequently selling public posts or giving other personnel-related benefits to their subordinates. This illegal business in some localities and government agencies appears to be highly rationally operated, with standardized prices and almost always swift delivery of the benefits. Just as the objective of *profiting* from illicit activities (e.g., drug, sex, and gambling) distinguishes organized crime from terrorism (Roth & Sever 2007), the bribees' main goal in an office-selling syndicate is often to further their economic interests. This economically oriented goal marks a major distinction from oligarchical power bases, which carry a political agenda besides seeking wealth. Many office buyers in office-selling syndicates resemble customers of organized crime, simply paying money for what they want (e.g., promotion, jobs) without clear signs of sharing common political goals with the office seller.

A prototypical example of an office-selling syndicate is the long office-selling chain in Heilongjiang province described in my earlier research (Zhu 2008). Han Guizhi, the minister of the provincial Department of Organization (DOO), sold several positions at the prefectural level, including the position of Party secretary of Suihua municipality, which was given to Ma De. Subsequently, Ma sold a series of positions at the county level, including the position of Party secretary of Suiling county, which went to Li Gang. Li Gang then sold many positions within his jurisdiction. Because so many officials and positions were involved in this office-selling chain, the investigation of the case in 2002 had cascading effects. Nevertheless, some office buyers "slipped through the net" and continued to receive promotions. One of them was Li Chuncheng, who bribed Han when working in Haerbin in the 1990s and was later transferred to Sichuan province, becoming a core member of Zhou Yongkang's clique.[12] This also indicates that the influence of a large office-selling syndicate may extend beyond its locality and over time.

The DOO leaders can conveniently engage in office-selling because these departments play an important role in personnel decisions, such as nominating, evaluating, and reviewing candidates. Local DOOs rank eleventh in the top twenty sectors of high tendencies of personnel corruption in Section 2. Several office sellers in Datasets A and B were heads or deputy heads of DOOs. For instance, Cui Zongxing was the head of a county-level DOO in Shandong province. He took bribes from sixty-seven people, some of whom bribed him once for multiple favors, while others bribed him multiple times for different personnel issues. He received more than eighty bribes for diverse favors, ranging from promotions and higher salaries to favorable performance reviews, vying for positions (*jingzheng shanggang*) and the removal of punishment records. The boxplot in Figure 13 integrates the types of favors (on the x-axis), the distribution of bribes equivalent in cash for each kind of favor (on the y-axis), and the frequencies of favors (in brackets) to demonstrate the wide spectrum of personnel issues in which a local DOO head could intervene and the large sums collected. Appearing thirty-five times, promotions were the most sought-after. The average price for promotion was similar to that of rotation within the work unit, the second most popular favor, and slightly cheaper than receiving both a promotion and better assessment results.

Another office-selling chain involving a DOO occurred in Danjiangkou, a prefectural-level municipality of Hubei province. Piecing together different court judgments related to this case sheds additional light on how an office-selling syndicate is operated as an ongoing enterprise and rationally for profit. Zhou, the former deputy head of the municipal DOO, took bribes from thirty-two people, who held low ranks in diverse government departments and public organizations. As shown in Figure 14, a relatively large number of the buyers were vice Party secretaries of townships, taxation bureaus, civil affairs, and

[12] See https://m.21jingji.com/article/20140430/herald/0aa43d3baf48f9e7ef99a2eb9d364e58.html.

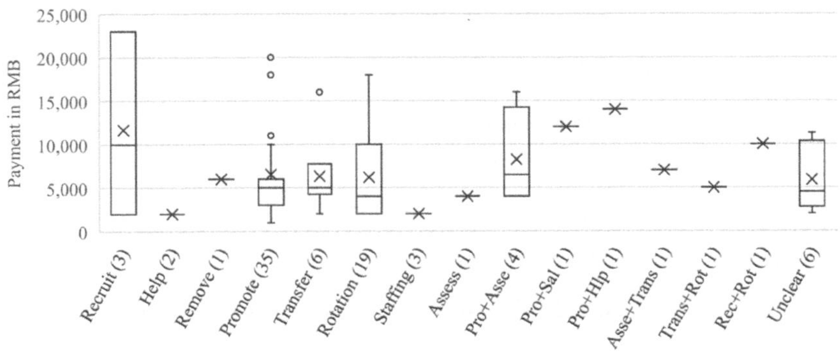

Figure 13 Boxplot payment collected by a county DOO head.

Note: (a) Each box shows the 25th to 75th percentiles of the amount of money taken by Cui; the short line within the box is the median, and "x" denotes the mean. (b) x-axis shows the favor types and their frequencies (in parentheses): Recruit = recruitment; Help = offering generic assistance (*guanzhao*); Remove = removing punishment; Promote = promotion; Transfer = lateral transfer to other departments; Rotation = rotation within work units; Staffing = leadership team staffing; Assess = assessment; Pro+Asse = promotion + assessment; Pro+Sal = promotion + increase salary; Pro+Hlp = promotion + help; Asse+Trans = assessment + transfer; Trans+Rot = transfer + rotation within; Rec+Rot = recruitment + rotation within; Unclear = no clear indication of favors. (c) One bribe not included in the figure involved RMB180,131 to help an individual to obtain a job and a contract for an orchard.

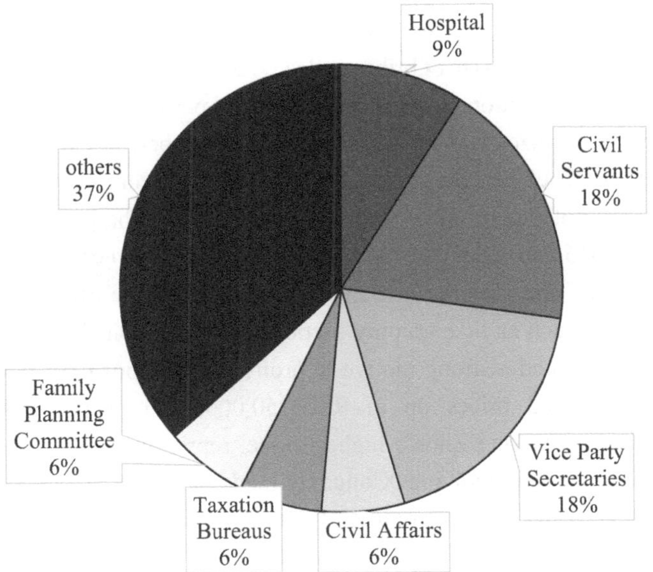

Figure 14 Sectoral distribution of positions sold by a deputy head of a municipal DOO.

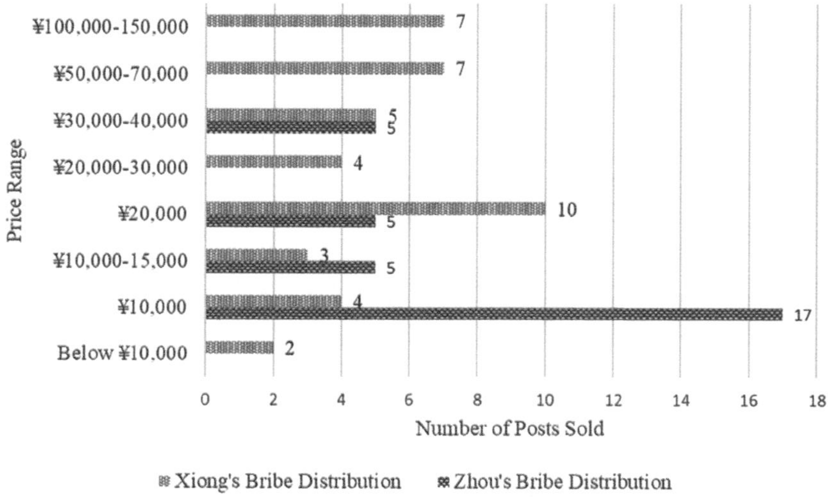

Figure 15 Price rationalization of office-selling cases in Hubei province.

hospitals. Sixteen sought promotions, thirteen asked for a change of positions within their agencies, one sought a higher salary, and another one bribed Zhou regarding leadership staffing. Office buyers with such diverse origins were able to perpetuate the office-selling syndicate by selling positions within their jurisdictions. One example was Xiong Tao, who spent RMB40,000 to purchase the head post of a major hospital in Danjiangkou and then sold forty-eight positions (e.g., doctors, nurses, and administrative posts) within the hospital.

A comparison of the size of bribes collected by Zhou and Xiong shows a clear tendency for price rationalization. The prices of posts handled by Zhou were relatively standardized and stable, largely remaining between RMB10,000 and RMB40,000. The average price charged for a promotion was around RMB16,154, not much higher than the average price charged for a position change, RMB15,556. There was no significant price difference between posts of different ranks, probably because the ranks sought by the office buyers were generally low, such as *fuke* (deputy section) or *ke* (section) level. In contrast, Xiong demonstrated a strong motive to profit from the positions bought from Zhou. He charged prices up to RMB150,000, and posts purchased for RMB50,000, surpassing Zhou's highest price, represented more than 29% of the forty-eight cases involving Xiong. He made at least RMB1,800,660 from office-selling, with a net profit of RMB1,760,660, excluding the money spent on purchasing the position of hospital head. Figure 15 compares the pricing structure of Zhou's and Xiong's office-selling "businesses" to illustrate the rationalization of prices.

Office-selling syndicates can create peer pressure that coerces individuals to follow suit, turning buying offices into a rule. Liu Chunmao, a county-level Party secretary in Shaanxi province, was involved in nineteen bribery cases. Some officials bribed him merely to maintain a good relationship with him and secure his support at work, such that Liu would not object when they were nominated for a promotion or promoted. Although no positions were directly sold in such cases, bribery became a prerequisite for smoothly obtaining a promotion. This suggests that bribery was an unspoken rule in the locality. Another interesting detail of Liu's case is that he spent all of his corrupt proceeds, RMB3.8 million, on lottery tickets and game credits.

Another example is a recent high-profile office-selling syndicate in Liaoning province. Purchasing for promotion and buying votes in elections had been popular for several years in the province. Many provincial- and municipal-level leaders were involved, either actively or passively. For instance, Su Hongzhang, a municipal leader seeking promotion, sent gold bars and iPhones to his superiors, who had the power to vote him onto the provincial standing committee. Another leader, Liu Qiang, realized that he had been passed over by Su for a vice-provincial position because he had not paid bribes; as a result, he decided to send larger amounts of money in future.[13] The massive political power and extensive network of high-level officials involved in this case are also common in oligarchical power bases.

3.4 Oligarchical Power Bases

Oligarchical power bases involve complicated personal networks in which political power and wealth are closely intertwined. Oligarchs are individuals who possess material power with the intention of "wealth defense and a motive of wealth accumulation," based on the rationale that the more resources one possesses, the more one strives to defend them (Winters 2011, p. 20). The politics of wealth defense can result in different forms of oligarchies (e.g., warring, ruling, sultanistic, and civil oligarchies) depending on the "nature of the threats to wealth and property and how the central problem of wealth defense is managed politically" (Winters 2011, p. 7). Politicians who are "corrupt and [have] amassed personal fortunes" can be considered ruling oligarchs (Winters 2011, p. 9).

I argue that many Chinese officials, especially those at high levels, who are involved in office-selling and charged by the CCP for engaging in "interest conveyance" (*liyi shusong* 利益输送) and "political disloyalty," belong to politician-transformed oligarchs and form oligarchical power bases through

[13] CCDI documentary www.youtube.com/watch?v=Y9ymGN7MkJg.

selling offices. These officials were initially empowered by their offices in the Party-state, enabling them to utilize their political influence to amass immense wealth through corrupt practices. To secure their benefits and counter threats (primarily from fellow oligarchs and those higher up), these oligarchs need to engage diligently in what I call "double defense" (Zhu 2022); that is, the defense of wealth and political power by broadening one's connections in both areas. Selling offices is not just a means of securing economic interests but also an instrument to help office sellers build cliques and secure advantages in intraparty elite power competition. This conscious double defense separates oligarchical power bases from primitive bribery, evolved bribery, and even office-selling syndicates, which are predominantly economically oriented. Oligarchical members' intention and ability to engage in double defense may jeopardize the stability of the regime and the position of their superiors, including the central leadership. Representative examples are Zhou Yongkang's corruption empire and Ling Jihua's Xishan Society.

Zhou Yongkang's corruption empire spanned the Chinese political economy. His advancement from the petroleum industry to Sichuan province, the politico-legal system, and eventually the PSC allowed him to build an extensive and far-reaching network, exemplifying a ruling oligarch's political power protection. He maintained relationships with his followers even when moving to different roles, a common strategy for preserving political resources. Simultaneously, Zhou sold offices to further expand his power. Many (vice-)ministerial/provincial-level officials that Zhou promoted or helped with promotions, such as Jiang Jiemin of the China National Petroleum Corporation, Li Chuncheng in Sichuan, Bai Enpei in Yunnan, and Zhou Benshun in Hebei, bribed him directly and/or transferred economic interests to his family members. For instance, Bai Enpei, former Party secretary of Yunnan, reportedly bribed Zhou and helped Zhou's son, Zhou Bin, acquire a local mine in exchange for Bai's further career advancement. Zhou Bin owned thirty-seven companies in oil production, hydroelectric power, real estate, asset management, and tourism. While most of these businesses were located in Sichuan, Zhou Yongkang's primary geographical power base, some extended operations to North American oil fields with the help of Zhou's petroleum gangs. The Zhou family amassed wealth mainly by placing pressure on individuals who owed their political careers or business successes to Zhou. Moreover, many of Zhou Yongkang's followers had their own followers. The recursive nature of this power protection amplified its expansion. Figure 16 illustrates the intersecting political and economic arenas of Zhou's oligarchical power base.

In contrast with Zhou Yongkang, whose wide entrenchment across the Chinese government matrix gave birth to his power base, Ling Jihua reached power

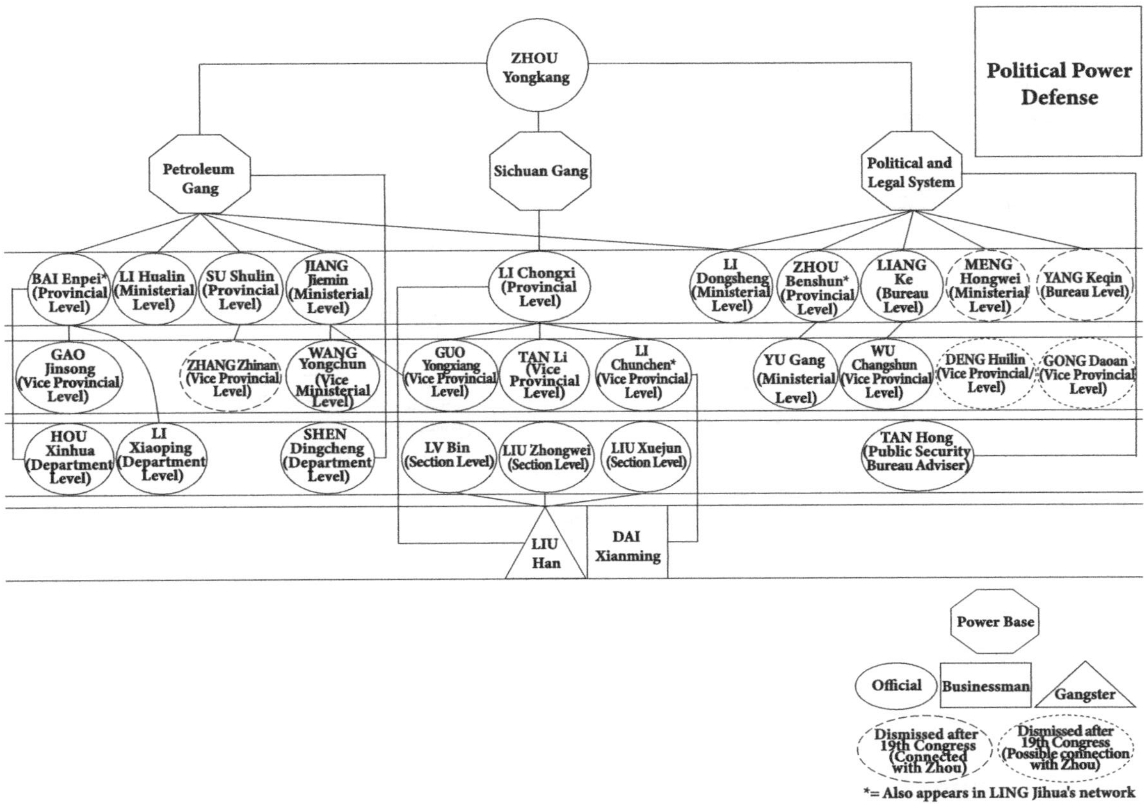

Figure 16a Zhou Yongkang's oligarchical power base.

Note: Officials are listed in layers based on their administrative rankings from the top down. Not all of the officials in the chart are discussed, due to space limits.

Source: Zhu (2022).

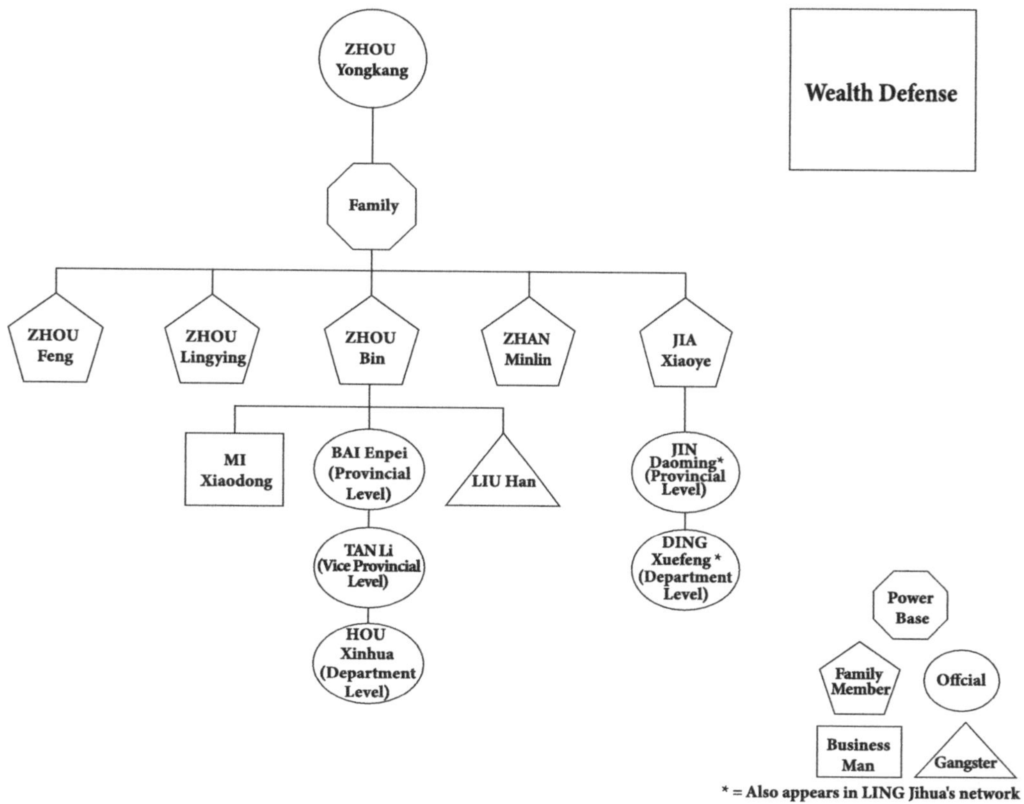
Wealth Defense
ZHOU Yongkang
Family
ZHOU Feng
ZHOU Lingying
ZHOU Bin
ZHAN Minlin
JIA Xiaoye
MI Xiaodong
BAI Enpei (Provincial Level)
LIU Han
JIN Daoming* (Provincial Level)
TAN Li (Vice Provincial Level)
DING Xuefeng * (Department Level)
HOU Xinhua (Department Level)
Power Base
Family Member
Offcial
Business Man
Gangster
* = Also appears in LING Jihua's network

Figure 16b

through the Communist Youth League. The trust placed in him by the former general secretary Hu Jintao was Ling's major political capital. The most important vehicle for Ling to amass political power and wealth was the Xishan Society, a tightly knit informal organization that expanded to protect Ling from potential political crises. It emerged in around 2007, when Ling ascended to leadership positions in the General Office and Central Secretariat, and functioned as a clandestine group of high-ranking officials and affluent businessmen originating from Shanxi province. Officials utilized the Society as a platform for bidding, purchasing, and selling offices, while businessmen funded the gatherings and consequently gained access to high-level authorities. For example, Chen Chuanping, a member of the Shanxi Provincial Party Committee and Party secretary of Taiyuan Municipality, who also hailed from Ling's hometown, accepted bribes to facilitate Liu Suiji's promotion to police chief. Similar practices of appointing and promoting fellow townsmen, friends, and family members to positions in local and national governments and SOEs occurred often within the Society. This not only showcased Ling's political influence but also enhanced his standing among aspiring cadres seeking promotions. Ling's wife, Gu Liping, extended Ling's connections by forming her own organizations. By promoting her nonprofit business associations, Gu fostered relationships with local officials and businessmen, including Bai Enpai and Li Chuncheng, who were central figures in Zhou Yongkang's network. In exchange for favors, they offered bribes to Ling through Gu, amounting to RMB600,000 and RMB890,000, respectively (Figure 17).

Many former high-level officials in Dataset A were either the center of their own oligarchical bases, members of the mega tigers' power bases, or both. Oligarchical power bases also exist at lower administrative levels, often centered around local governors, Party secretaries, or leaders of resourceful units such as public security or finance sectors. They were like "little Zhou" or "little Ling" within their local jurisdictions. For instance, Wang Sihua, a former county Party secretary of Jiangxi province, was charged with political showmanship ostensibly while building up his cliques within the government by displaying favoritism and cronyism in personnel matters. He arranged for Li, who had a long record of misconduct, to become a township Party secretary; promoted Zhao, who had behaved poorly in the past, to county Party committee member without following the standard procedure (*poge tiba*); and raised Huang, who had bribed Wang and his wife, rapidly through the ranks. Under such an atmosphere, many officials competed to demonstrate loyalty to Wang and bribe him and his family. Wang's political influence was exploited by his brother, who received bribes totaling RMB5.4 million from

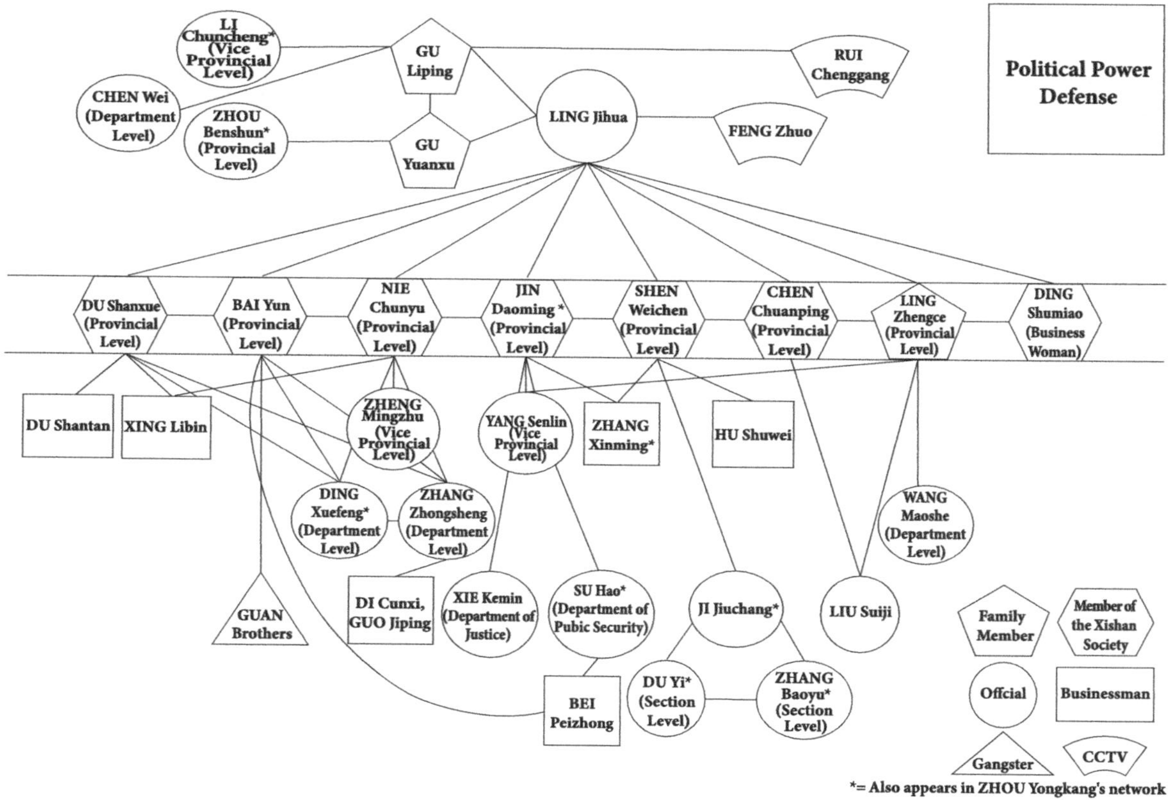

Figure 17a Ling Jihua's oligarchical power base.

Note: Same as in Figure 16.
Source: Zhu (2022).

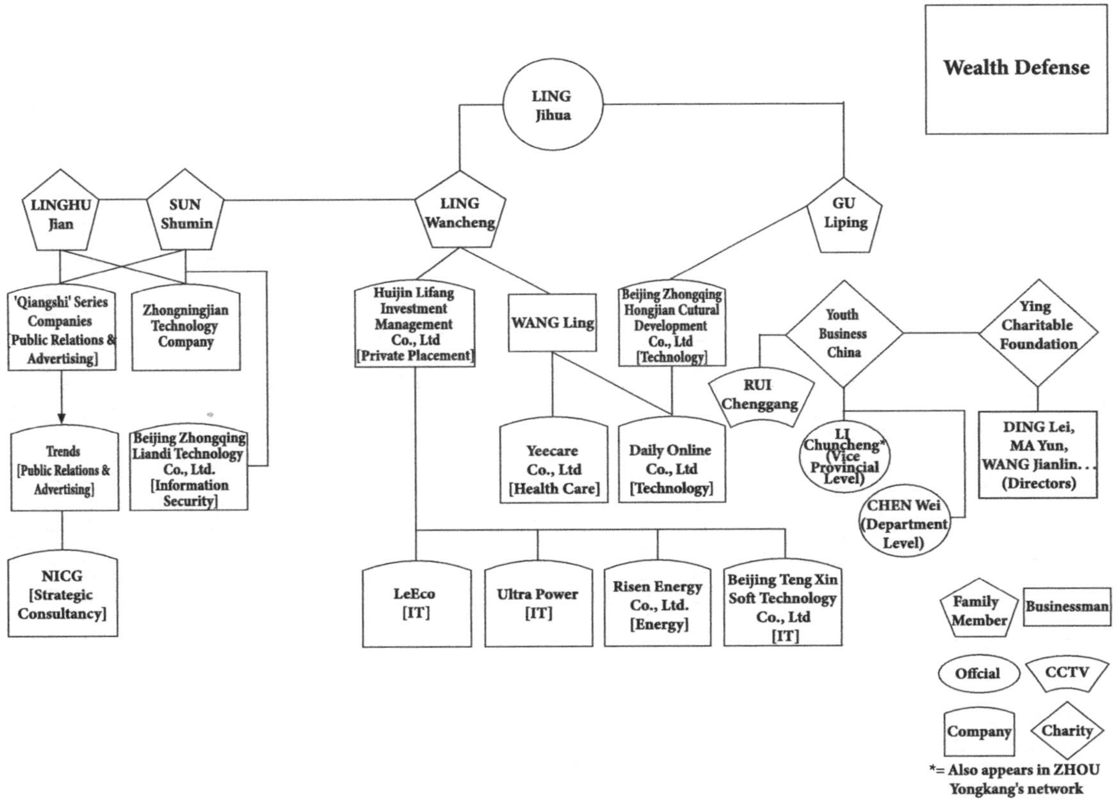

Wealth Defense
LING Jihua
LINGHU Jian
SUN Shumin
LING Wancheng
GU Liping
'Qiangshi' Series Companies [Public Relations & Advertising]
Zhongningjian Technology Company
Huijin Lifang Investment Management Co., Ltd [Private Placement]
WANG Ling
Beijing Zhongqing Hongjian Cutural Development Co., Ltd [Technology]
Youth Business China
Ying Charitable Foundation
RUI Chenggang
Trends [Public Relations & Advertising]
Beijing Zhongqing Liandi Technology Co., Ltd. [Information Security]
Yeecare Co., Ltd [Health Care]
Daily Online Co., Ltd [Technology]
LI Chuncheng* (Vice Provincial Level)
CHEN Wei (Department Level)
DING Lei, MA Yun, WANG Jianlin. . . (Directors)
NICG [Strategic Consultancy]
LeEco [IT]
Ultra Power [IT]
Risen Energy Co., Ltd. [Energy]
Beijing Teng Xin Soft Technology Co., Ltd [IT]
Family Member
Businessman
Offcial
CCTV
Company
Charity
*= Also appears in ZHOU Yongkang's network

Figure 17b

several individuals to obtain advantages in bidding for construction projects and promotions.[14]

Another example of a lower-level oligarchical power base is Jiang Zhaogang, who was denounced by the CCP for violating political rules, extensively practicing political sycophancy (*dagao zhengzhi panfu*), and establishing cliques.[15] Jiang aligned himself with Cao Jianfang, a former member of the Yunnan Provincial Party Committee and vice-governor, who facilitated his promotion to Party secretary of the Provincial Rural Credit Union (PRCN) in 2011. Jiang willingly served as an instrument for Cao's corruption and started to engage in rampant office-selling. He placed his relatives and cronies in key roles in various departments of the PRCN. This strategy solidified his power base in the PRCN, making it easier for him to obtain and distribute benefits, such as providing help and seeking advantages for others in loan processing, enterprise financing, and project contracting. He received RMB27 million in bribes through his wife, his mistress, and his mistress's mother. Under Jiang's tenure, the PRCN became his kingdom.

3.5 Dynamic Relations of the Four Types of Sale of Offices

The discussion in the previous sections illustrates the office-selling and buying process. One remaining issue concerns the commitment of those selling official positions: How can bribers be ensured that these sellers will genuinely support their advancement after receiving the money? What if they renege? As one interviewed anticorruption agent half-jokingly remarked:

> The credibility of such commitments largely depends on the character of the leader involved – ironic, perhaps, considering the context of corruption. Some officials 'get things done' and accept the money with a clear conscience, and some will return the money if they do not get it done. When people offer money but are not appointed, two outcomes are typically possible: One is that the person continues to 'invest' in the hope of being promoted next time; the other is a falling out that results in the briber reporting the leader who took the money. Cases are often exposed because someone paid for a position but did not get it.[16]

Additionally, although I theorize four types of buying and selling offices, they are not mutually exclusive; some cases could encompass several types. In practice, sometimes it may be difficult to distinguish between types, especially office-selling syndicates and oligarchical power bases. Some cases might occupy the intersections between different types. Relatively simple types can also evolve

[14] See www.163.com/dy/article/I38816BJ0553832F.html; https://m.thepaper.cn/kuaibao_detail.jsp?contid=4236164&from=kuaibao.

[15] See www.sohu.com/a/274006491_391599.

[16] Interview conducted in June 2025.

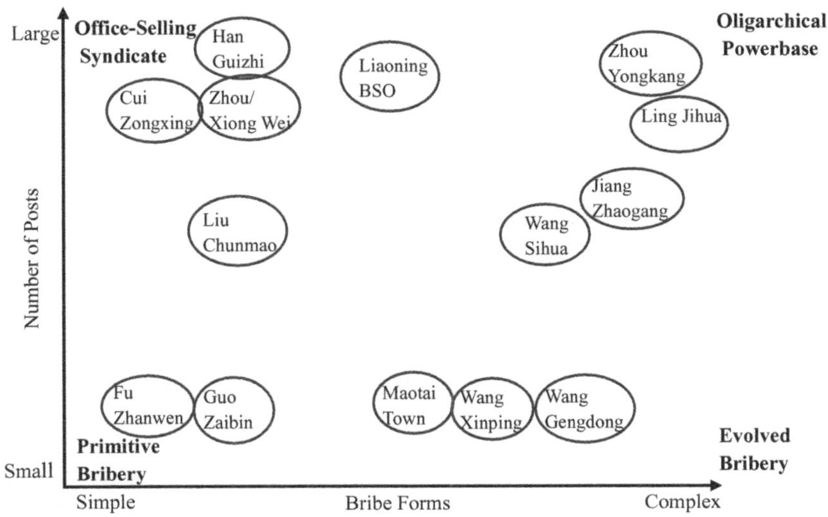

Figure 18 Mapping types of buying and selling offices in continuous dimensions.

Note: BSO means buying and selling offices.

into more complex types if corruption is not effectively controlled. Thus, we can consider the two dimensions as two axes of continuous instead of discrete variables. I map the examples discussed in the previous sections in Figure 18.

I also systematically categorize the cases in Dataset B through a close reading of the court judgments to identify a "rule of thumb" for different types of office-selling at lower administrative levels, based on proportions, distribution across bureaucratic levels, temporal dynamics, and enforcement risks. The results may be subject to selection bias and missing information (for example, complex networks of people buying offices may not be revealed in the judgments, such that certain seemingly "primitive" cases could in fact involve more complex networks) and should thus be interpreted with caution. First, 38% of the cases involve primitive bribery, 17% constitute evolved bribery, 50% are office-selling syndicates, and 3% involve oligarchical power bases. This means that more than half of the cases involve the sale of multiple positions and are relatively well organized, with implicit rules. Moreover, at least thirty-two cases by the counts of court judgments involve the sale of more than twenty positions; the largest involves a school head selling school admissions to 104 students, followed by the previously discussed case of Cui Zongxing, a county DOO head.

Second, although I detect no correlation between office-selling types and bureaucratic levels, the "first-hand" of a local jurisdiction or a work unit is more likely than others to be involved in selling multiple positions. The

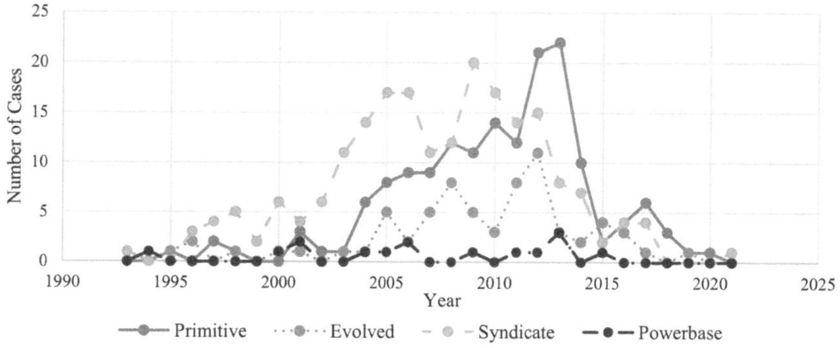

Figure 19 The first year of occurrence of the four types of cases.

percentages of first-hands being office sellers in primitive bribery, evolved bribery, office-selling syndicates, and oligarchical power bases are 63.8%, 54.9%, 73.9%, and 87.5%, respectively. The immense decision-making power held by the first hands enables them to sell multiple positions; moreover, these leaders tend to have more political ambitions to form power bases than other leaders, in addition to seeking economic interests. In addition, and consistent with other discussions in this section, I find that DOO heads involved in selling offices are most likely to engage in syndicates. Seven out of ten cases involving DOO heads in Dataset B belong to office-selling syndicates.

Third, I examine the first year when a case occurs for each of the four types to identify temporal dynamics. Figure 19 shows slightly different but generally similar trends for the four types. While all types slowly increase from the mid 1990s to the early 2000s, the peak for office-selling syndicates occurs between 2005 and 2010, evolved and primitive bribery continue to increase until 2012 and 2013, respectively, and oligarchical power bases exhibit a generally flat trend due to their small number. This trend is consistent with the general intensification of corruption during the 1990s and 2000s observed by other scholars (Wedeman 2022). The lag between the decline of office-selling syndicates and those of evolved and primitive bribery, which increased until 2012 and 2013, respectively, could be due to Xi's corruption crackdown, which stopped many office-selling cases in their early stages from developing into more serious types.

Finally, enforcement risk varies by type. The average latency periods for primitive bribery, evolved bribery, office-selling syndicates, and oligarchical power bases, respectively, are 4.6, 5.8, 8.4, and 7.3 years. Thus, corruption sophistication is not monotonically positively correlated with exposure risk. Office-selling syndicates and oligarchical power bases inherently take longer to build up, but their latency periods indicate that selling more offices does not make an office seller more likely to be exposed. Instead, the complex types are more effectively organized and more likely to routinize office-selling, making bribery an important contributor to cadres' career advancement. Overall, the comparison of subtypes shows that while money, or capital, binds parties, buying and selling offices occur in distinct ways and in the service of different economic and political agendas. In Section 5, I utilize subtype characteristics to map promotions by purchasing office to the tripartite framework of political selection, and I examine the subtypes' relationship with economic growth in Section 6.

4 Causes: Why Is Buying and Selling Offices Possible?

Personnel corruption is caused by multiple factors, several of which also apply to corruption in general. I summarize the primary causes of personnel corruption at the structural and agent levels in Table 4. Structural-level causes affect most individuals and define the general environment to which agents must adapt. Agent-level causes are the subjective viewpoints and motives of individual actors, whose impact on actors' engagement in buying and selling offices can vary greatly between individuals. "Agents" primarily include cadres working in the government and other public sectors and can extend to their relatives and entrepreneurs. In addition, some causes in Table 4 create opportunities for personnel corruption, while others incentivize agents to engage in it. Instances of office sales can also reinforce themselves as informal rules, which I define as "the order of office-selling." This order can generate enormous peer pressure, be taken for granted, and be "automatically" followed by agents (Kaufmann, Pradhan, & Ryterman 1998). In addition to several previously discussed causes, I propose that the rejuvenation of the cadre corps in China has put pressure on officials to seek promotions at the earliest opportunity. Many cadres even pay bribes to "jump the queue" (*chadui*).

4.1 Cadre Management as an Opportunity for Personnel Corruption

The CCP's cadre management system, derived partly from the Soviet Union's nomenklatura system, allowed the CCP to concentrate its power in the hands of a selected few. This created an important foundation for maintaining the regime's strength. However, several components of this system have offered opportunities for buying and selling offices, especially the "one-level-down" management reform, ambiguous promotion criteria, and power concentration in the decision-making process.

Table 4 Main causes of buying and selling offices

	Structural-level Causes	Agent-level Causes
Opportunities	• The formal cadre-promotion system and procedure, e.g., decentralization of personnel management, power concentration in the political selection process, loopholes for exploitation. • Weak cadre-monitoring system and law enforcement.	• Private entrepreneurs' need for connections with government officials provides resources for bribes. • Personal network, e.g., family and friends, as extended instruments of corruption.
Incentives	• Age ceiling of promotion. • Importance of personal relationships to informal politics (discussed in Section 5).	• Career aspirations, e.g., for more power, higher political and economic returns at higher government positions.

Order: Purchasing offices can generate peer pressure, leading more cadres to follow suit.

Low Risk Nature: Office buyers and sellers share the risk of punishment.

Cycle: Buying and selling offices expands from the bottom up and the top down as participants' connections expand with their career advancement and their followers gain followers.

4.1.1 One-Level-Down Management

Since the 1950s, the cadre management system has evolved into a hierarchical and controlled form (Manion 2023). The introduction of the "one-level-down" principle in 1984 further solidified the hierarchical stratification of power and fostered an environment conducive to office sales, because it spread the power of appointing officials more broadly throughout the government hierarchy (Zhu 2008). Each level of the state apparatus was granted the power to appoint, promote, transfer, and dismiss government officials at the level immediately below. This decentralization process gave local governments more agency in personnel management, becoming the primary driver of sale of offices, especially at and below the county level (Pei 2016). The rise of illicit office-selling markets began in the 1990s onwards, as verified in my Dataset B. Pei (2016) also argues that the limited geographical scope of lower-level governments helps potential buyers to gain important knowledge, such as who to bribe and the prices of positions, and get in touch with office sellers, such as the county Party chief. This argument was echoed by local prosecutors that I interviewed, and in Dataset B, at least 25% of the cases occurred at and below the county level. However, more than 80% of the high-ranking officials in Dataset A were involved in buying and selling offices, indicating that intense personnel corruption can also occur at high levels of government.

4.1.2 Ambiguous Promotion Criteria

In theory, cadres are evaluated by a formalized set of standards increasingly strengthened by the cadre management system. The standards are closely tied to the target responsibility system, which was introduced in the early economic reform era. Officials sign contracts obliging them to achieve certain performance targets, which are weighed differently depending on the context of posts and local governance priorities (Edin 1998, 2003; Whiting 2001, 2004). Additional criteria were formulated in 1995 to assess township and county leaders, and a regulation to monitor compliance with formal appointment procedures was issued in 2001 (Chan & Gao 2008; Zhu 2008; Manion 2023). The criteria for evaluating and promoting officials have since extended beyond target fulfillment. The five main formal evaluation criteria are virtue (*de* 德), organizational ability and leadership (*neng* 能), industriousness (*qin* 勤), policy accomplishment (*ji* 绩), and integrity (*lian* 廉) (Manion 1985; Zeng & Wong 2021). Emphasis is usually placed on policy accomplishment, digitized as economic growth and GDP. Officials are compared with their peers, and the results may affect their bonus and promotion opportunities.

In practice, tightened assessment could trigger bribery to obtain better evaluation results. Moreover, inconsistencies in promotional decisions deviate from the formal criteria. Some consider more holistic leadership qualities, such as "virtue, effort, and integrity" (Manion 2023, p. 60), to be prevalent additional criteria. The subjectivity of these factors makes it relatively easy to manipulate cadre evaluation, as they are difficult to quantify. Manion (2023) considers the selection procedure to involve continuous observation of preselected candidates and their nomination to be dependent on the time and place once a vacancy arises. This leaves room to justify bribery-induced promotions through subjective criteria and the specific context of an individual working position. Landry, Lü, and Duan (2018) also suggest that good performance is less likely to lead to promotions at higher levels of government. Especially in senior positions, this gap in formal criteria may leave room for other promotion-influencing activities, such as buying and selling offices.

4.1.3 Power Concentration

The power of political selection and decision-making is concentrated with the few leaders heading a Party committee, such as the Party secretary, governor of a local government or functional department, and head of the local DOO. This power dynamic can easily be exploited, enabling the decision-makers to sell offices and making bribery targets more easily identifiable within a small circle of superiors (Zhu 2008).

At all levels of the state hierarchy, one must be nominated by the Party secretary and DOO head. The Central Organization Department (COD) is one of the highest-level institutions, extending much power to its leading members. Its ministers oversee the selection of provincial Party and government leaders and are responsible for "nomination, evaluation, candidate review, and the *bei'an zhidu* (system of reporting for the record)" (Zhu 2008, p. 561). Other leaders are also allowed to propose candidates to compete for votes, a practice especially encouraged in the 1980s (Manion 1985; Pei 2016). This means that officials bribed can leverage personal recommendations for office buyers. The Party secretary has especially great discretion; in Party committee meetings, other officials usually avoid opposing top leaders' decisions, as this could risk their favored candidates' being vetoed by the Party secretary. For instance, in the vote-buying case in Liaoning province discussed in Section 3, Wang Min, the provincial Party secretary, proposed Su Hongzhang as a candidate for election to the provincial Party committee, which was decisive in Su's promotion to a vice-provincial post. Li Tiecheng, a county Party secretary, admitted to having rejected candidate shortlists if the DOO did not include applicants who had bribed him (Pei 2016).

The political selection procedure also lacks transparency, creating loopholes and opportunities for manipulation. As promotion relies on the moods of superiors, paying bribes could be considered an attempt to appease them (Sun 2004). Cadres working for the DOO can hamper the sequence of candidate nominations or erase records from a candidate's file that could tarnish their reputability (Zhu 2008). The vote-buying case in Liaoning province also shows that the COD's screening of promotion candidates cannot effectively scrutinize problematic candidates. The collective decision-making process also shields individuals from being held accountable for selling offices. All promotional decisions must be passed unanimously by the Party committee; therefore, responsibility cannot be easily traced back to one person (Zhu 2008). This also makes it more difficult to gather hard evidence for court cases (Pei 2016).

4.2 Ineffective Monitoring

China's anticorruption system has taken various forms, from a tripartite design in the 1990s to the dual supervision of the CCDI as the Party-state's disciplinary apparatus and the procuratorate as its legal apparatus, and, more recently, a centralized supervisory system under the National Supervision Commission.

Nevertheless, the CCDI, together with its lower branches, the CDIs, has always been the leading anticorruption agency in contemporary China. Thus, the institutional design of the CCDI hierarchy greatly influences the effectiveness of efforts to curb corruption in China.

4.2.1 Lack of Reliable Reports of Personnel Corruption

As corruption is usually secret, anticorruption agencies find it difficult to collect concrete evidence. It can be even more difficult to obtain reliable reports of buying and selling offices, due to the collusive nature of this kind of corruption. Bribers are usually more incentivized to report extortive corruption, because they are blackmailed to pay bribes, than collusive corruption, which benefits both sides, giving parties little incentive to report it (Brunetti & Weder 2003). In the sale of office, once a "pay-and-promote" transaction is concluded, the office buyer and seller tend to share both the benefits of career advancement and the risk of detection.

Moreover, stringent requirements for evidence to initiate a case filing in China can further discourage the reporting of corruption. According to Guo (2014), CCDI's workflow on a case consists of eight steps: preliminary evidence and complaint management; preliminary confirmation of disciplinary violations; approval for opening the case; investigation and evidence collection; case hearing; implementation of disciplinary sanctions; appeal by the disciplined official; and continued supervision and management of the case. To successfully file a complaint against an official, the report must show clear and persuasive evidence confirming their disciplinary violations (i.e., step 2). Real names are also needed to facilitate verification when reporting senior officials (Zhu 2008). However, informants are rarely willing to use real names, due to concerns about retaliation. This demonstrates the importance of protecting whistleblowers and public trust in anticorruption agencies.[17] Due to the lack of evidence, many cases are only accidentally uncovered and formally filed many years later. The long latency period of many cases allows for the continuous growth of the office-selling order, dragging more officials into its whirlpool, as in Heilongjiang, Liaoning, and Shanxi.

4.2.2 Dependency on Local Governments

To strengthen the supervision of local government, dual leadership was introduced to the CDI system in 1982 and further reinforced in 1992 by revising the

[17] Most corruption reports contain real names in Hong Kong (Scott & Gong 2015; Xiao, Gong, & Tu 2024).

Party Constitution. Before the reform, a local CDI was fully subordinate to the local Party group, which controlled its budget and assessed its performance, leaving the CDI nearly incapable of supervising the local Party committee. The CDI officials may also be reluctant to open cases against their colleagues unless requested to do so by higher authorities (Guo 2014). Under the dual leadership reform, every local CDI is also under the leadership of the CDI one level up. Thus, when a local CDI disagrees with the decisions of its leading Party committee at the same level, the agency is authorized to ask the CDI one level higher to reexamine the case. However, if a local CDI reports an office buying case higher up, the higher-level CDI head is only one voting member of the higher-level Party committee. Multiple committee members can influence decision-making and the Party secretary usually has the final say in investigation decisions. If any Party committee member, including the Party secretary, were involved in the corruption case in question (e.g., as an office seller), they could obstruct the CDI's investigation initiative. Thus, office-selling cases are relatively unlikely to be uncovered and investigated.

Research also shows that only a small percentage of officials are referred to legal procedures for legal penalties (e.g., Gong & Li 2019). The severity of penalties, instead of being solely determined by the legality of a case, tends to vary by political concerns, such as defendants' former positions and public attention to a case (Zhu 2015; Chen & Li 2024). The considerable judicial discretion and sentencing disparities may further compromise the legal deterrence of corruption.

4.3 Age Ceiling as an Incentive to Pay for Promotion

A less frequently discussed structural-level cause motivating paying for promotion is the age ceiling on Chinese officials' advancement trajectory. To accelerate China's modernization, the CCP gradually adjusted the composition of leadership groups at all levels to form a younger, better-educated, and more highly skilled force (Manion 1985). Age restrictions on promotion were implemented in the 1980s. Meanwhile, rigid appointment mechanisms uphold order and stability by ensuring step-by-step career progress and preventing the chaotic and unregulated promotions that occurred during the Cultural Revolution (Kou & Tsai 2014). Party provisions regulate cadre tenures, specifically mandating a fixed five-year tenure for each cadre position.[18] Tension between these conflicting principles has created a dilemma for Chinese officials, who seek fast promotion whenever possible before reaching the age limits, while

[18] Article 3 of the "Interim Provisions for Party and Government Leading Cadre Tenure," promulgated by the central authorities in 2006.

simultaneously being constrained by the gradual nature of career progression and lengthy official tenure (Kou & Tsai 2014). Aspiring CCP cadres are forced to pursue rapid advancement by all means to prevent early and irreversible career stagnation. Table 5, adapted from Kou and Tsai (2014), illustrates the age dilemma faced by different ranks.

The age ceiling is particularly pronounced at the county level, barring officials from upward promotion across administrative levels. Cadres' upward mobility

Table 5 Age dilemma in CCP cadre management system

	Position rank	**Age ceiling for promotion**	**Expected age of promotion under regulated tenure**
zheng guo (正国)	National Leader	67	75
fu guo (副国)	Deputy National Leader	67	70
zheng bu (正部)	Minister/ Provincial Leader	63	65
fu bu (副部)	Deputy Minister/ Vice-Provincial Leader	58	60
zheng ting (正厅)	Bureau Director/ Prefectural Leader	55	55
fu ting (副厅)	Deputy Bureau Director/Vice-Prefectural Leader	52	50
zheng chu (正处)	Division Head/ County Leader	50	45
fu chu (副处)	Deputy Division Head/Vice-County Leader	45	40
zheng ke (正科)	Section Head	40	35
fu ke (副科)	Deputy Section Head	40	30

Source: Adapted from Kou and Tsai (2014).

from the county to the municipal level is much lower than that between the municipal and provincial levels (Kosta & Yu 2015). Under the regular track, a cadre is expected to attain the post of bureau director at fifty-five, and no further promotion to higher ranks is possible after a five-year term. Once a cadre hits the age ceiling, they can only stay in their current position until retirement. Even when cadres have not reached the mandatory retirement age, they are eliminated from the candidate list once they surpass a specific age threshold. With a retirement age of fifty-five for county leaders, only leaders under forty-five are considered eligible to stay on the reserve list for potential advancement (Zhong 2015). Pieke (2009) finds that cadres who have not reached the division (*chu*) level by approximately forty should realistically not anticipate any further rank advancements. This bottleneck effect results in discontent and insecurity among cadres, as they have no opportunities to realize their potential (Pieke 2009).

Young cadres who are promoted earlier have more opportunities to prolong their careers (Guo 2009); therefore, officials are eager to fast-track their promotion. Under Deng Xiaoping, three fast-track routes were developed for cadres to circumvent the regular promotion track and strict tenure restrictions (Kou & Tsai 2014). The first route involves temporarily assigning cadres to the leading group of the Communist Youth League (CYL), where age limits are stricter than those in the regular government. After serving in the CYL, cadres are reassigned to equivalent government and Party positions, with massive age advantages over candidates on the regular track. The second method involves a temporary transfer of duty (*guazhi duanlian*), whereby cadres are assigned to take temporary posts by their initial unit for major projects or key tasks.[19] This allows cadres to gain experience and develop hard skills in practice before advancing to higher echelons. Their performance in the external unit is appraised (*jianding*), and cadres with outstanding results may be awarded an exceptional promotion (Tsai & Kou, 2015). This supports the finding (see Figure 8) that several cases in Dataset B involved bribery for more mobility opportunities. The third route is nonregulation promotion. According to Deng, "the progressive promotion pathway is out of fashion; instead we have to create a new platform for a breakthrough, exceptionally promoting young and excellent cadres."[20] Through this route, cadres can be promoted before they complete the fixed length of tenure (*poge tiba*) or by "leap-frog promotion" (*yueji tiba*), enabling them to skip an entire rank on the career ladder (Kostka & Yu 2015; Wu 2015; Pang, Keng, & Zhong 2018).

[19] Article 72 of "The Civil Servant Law of the People's Republic of China," promulgated in 2005. (www.gov.cn/flfg/2005-06/21/content_8249.htm)

[20] Deng Xiaoping, "Reform of the system of Party and state leadership" (1980). www.reformdata.org/1980/0818/15396.shtml.

In practice, nonregulation promotions leave much room for selling offices, because leaders wield great discretion in recommending and promoting candidates to the designated positions. Although "open selection" (*gongkai xuanba*) and "vying for appointment" (*jingzheng shanggang*) were introduced to enhance the transparency of the recruitment process, these measures have become common ways to bypass the regular promotion track (Doyon 2018, p. 100). "Open selection" refers to recruiting candidates externally, while "vying for appointment" means that candidates are selected internally among cadres. Both processes require the employer to publicly announce vacant positions, establish a procedure for all candidates who fulfill the necessary conditions to submit job applications, and select candidates through written exams and interviews. Paradoxically, these mechanisms have been criticized for their opaque assessment criteria and subjective interview standards, enabling leaders to circumvent the rigidities of step-by-step promotion. Several cases in Dataset B involve bribery during vying for appointments, including the case of Cui Zongxing mentioned in Section 3.

Recognizing the potential loopholes, the CCP has recently downplayed open selection and competitive appointments. For instance, no related provisions, including operational procedures and criteria, are featured in the updated 2019 Work Regulations.[21] However, this increasing obscurity may inadvertently provide more leeway for manipulation (Doyon 2018).

I examine the conjecture that the age ceiling on promotion incentivizes buying offices by analyzing office buyers' ages. Figure 20 illustrates the age

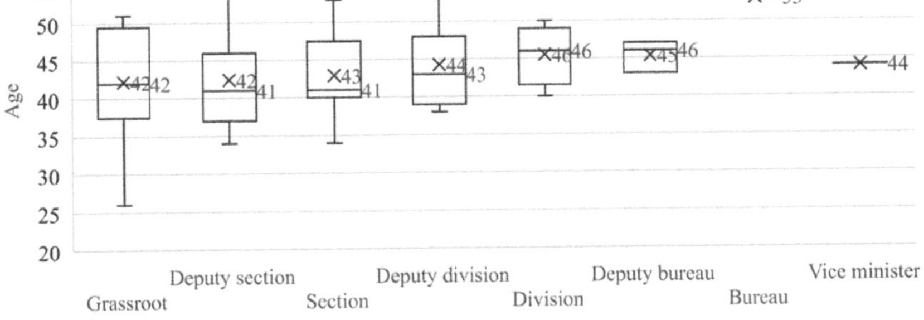

Figure 20 Boxplot of office buyers' ages by rank.

Note: The bar in box represents the median age; "X" is the average age.

[21] *Party and Government Leading Cadre Work Appointment Selection Regulations*, promulgated by the central authorities in 2019.

distribution of office buyers of different ranks.[22] On average, office buyers in Dataset B were relatively young – aged forty-two to forty-five. The median ages of all ranks except those at and below the *ke* (section) level are below the corresponding age ceilings for promotion in Table 5, indicating that at least half of all office buyers try to speed up their promotions by sending bribes. This urgency is especially salient for ranks at and above *chu* (division), as all the office buyers' ages were below the age ceiling in those cases. The general trend supports my hypothesis that many cadres attempt to use bribery to help them obtain early promotions for greater upward mobility.

I also examine the age of the office sellers to see whether a "retirement cliff," or the so-called "59 phenomenon" in many corruption cases (i.e., officials nearing retirement being more likely to engage in corruption to maximize their final rent-seeking opportunities), occurs in personnel corruption. I use boxplots to illustrate the distribution of the office sellers' ages when they first sell public positions across bureaucratic ranks. Figure 21 shows that the median age across ranks is approximately forty-five years and that 75% of the office sellers are roughly ten years younger than their retirement age of sixty years. At first glance, this finding contradicts the "59 phenomenon." However, as discussed, the ceiling interval for low- to mid-level officials falls between forty-five and fifty years. When sellers see diminishing opportunities for further promotion, they may have greater incentives to seek rents by utilizing their power, including power over political selection, to amass wealth or even to finance their own promotion as a last resort. Thus, the age ceiling for promotion pushes the retirement cliff earlier in officials'

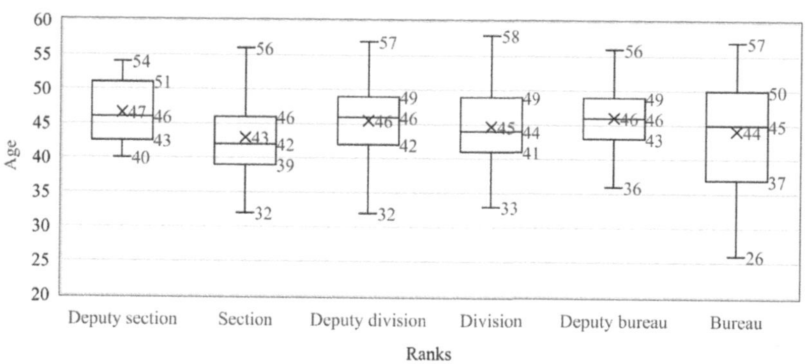

Figure 21 Boxplot of office sellers' age by rank.

Note: Same as Figure 20.

[22] The small sample size does not enable time series tests.

careers. This finding provides additional support for the correlation between the age ceiling and greater incentives to pay for promotion.

4.4 Agent-Level Causes of Buying and Selling Offices

4.4.1 "Campaign Finance" Sponsored by Entrepreneurs

Some cadres have more access to capital than others due to their closer relationships with entrepreneurs, who can provide them with funding to purchase government posts. As argued by Pearson, Rithmire, and Tsai (2023), China's political economy is a fusion of the developmental state, state capitalism, and elements of fascism, which has emerged as a response to the Party-state's prioritization of control, risk management, and political security. In such Party-state capitalism, the line between state and private ownership is blurred. Private entrepreneurs and government officials both need to build formal and informal connections. Private entrepreneurs need political protections to evade restrictions, access important resources (e.g., bank loans and land), and avoid occasional ideological attacks and political crackdowns (Kraus 1991; Tsai 2006). Local government officials rely on private entrepreneurs for tax revenue, local employment opportunities, assistance with meeting critical state goals, and personal wealth accumulation (Oi 1999; Whiting 2001; Edin 2003; Ang 2020). Scholars have coined different terms, such as "symbiotic relationship," "clientelist relationship," "organized clientelism," and "mutual endangerment," to characterize the dynamic mutual reliance between the two sides and their dependence on (in)formal platforms for enduring cooperation in different politico-economic contexts (e.g., Solinger 1992; Young 1995; Pearson 1997; Wank 2001; Dickson 2003; Sun, Zhu, & Wu 2014; Rithmire & Chen 2021; Zhang 2022).

Many private entrepreneurs consider paying to cultivate a close relationship with government officials an "investment." My interviewees remarked that businessmen are enthusiastic about building connections with officials at higher ranks or having ties at higher levels. Some businessmen can skillfully assess whether an official truly holds important positions or has extensive connections. Businessmen used the word *touta*, "investing upon him," when they thought the official was worth building connections with.[23] One interviewee reported that entrepreneurs sometimes "invested" continuously in officials if they saw them as having the potential for promotion, as the officials' career advancement would also benefit the entrepreneurs.[24]

Officials may also proactively solicit bribes from entrepreneurs to "finance" their promotion. Campaign financing is important for political candidates to win

[23] Interviews conducted in March 2024. [24] Interview conducted in October 2023.

elections in democracies, because to influence public voting decisions, electoral operations require immense financial resources to conduct political advertising, organize grassroots, and reach voters extensively (Freedman, Franz, & Goldstein 2004). With machine politics, political candidates can buy votes by directly paying voters with material goods (Scott 1969). Although the selectorate in China is often not the general public but a few top officials, bribing leaders can be considered campaign financing or direct vote buying with Chinese characteristics. In Liaoning province, Su Hongzhang and several other officials gave gold bars to members who could influence personnel decision-making. Large amounts of the capital came from local private entrepreneurs, who expected to benefit from Su's promotion in the future. Lu Enguang, a rural entrepreneur-turned-official, used his firm to "finance" every step of his promotion to vice-minister in the Department of Justice.[25] Because of the small size of the selectorate, votes can be bought relatively easily in the Chinese context.

4.4.2 Privatization of Public Power by Relatives

Officials' available personal networks also facilitate buying offices. Nathan and Tsai (1995) argue that Chinese political elites often form networks based on kinship or marriage. Close relatives privatize officials' public power and extend their influence. Government officials' associates, such as relatives, mistresses, and friends, often receive (send) bribes on their behalf or serve as intermediaries between office sellers and buyers. In Dataset B, many cadres visited leaders during major festivals, such as the Spring and Mid-autumn festivals, sending red packets to their children or other relatives, sometimes for consecutive years. Transfers of interest, in particular, tend to go through officials' relatives to legalize bribes. For instance, Bai Enpei transferred interest to Zhou Yongkang by supporting Zhou's son's businesses in Yunnan province.

4.4.3 Agents' Desire for Money and Power

Although mundane, the most direct incentive at the agent level is money. As shown in Section 3, returns on selling offices can be particularly high in office-selling syndicates. Office buyers with higher or more important positions can also earn more money by selling government positions themselves or through other types of corruption, as reflected in the uneven prices for political power, as previously discussed. An extreme example of officials' desire for monetary wealth is provided by Fu Jun, a county-level education bureau director in

[25] CCDI documentary, www.youtube.com/watch?v=khgH53ZmdtE&t=1831s.

Hainan province. He confessed to the judge that he had taken bribes not because he lacked money but simply because he enjoyed having money.[26]

Power, another motive for buying offices, determines the likelihood that an individual in a social relationship will achieve their desire, even with others' resistance (Best 2002). Power has two fundamental dimensions: possessing power and exercising power. An individual's ability to possess power derives from their ability to control various social resources, such as land, capital, social respect, physical strength, and knowledge. The ability to exercise power takes different forms, but all are intended to exert one's will despite others' resistance (Best 2002; Hurst 2007). The aim for power is most salient in oligarchical power bases, with "big tigers" corruptly uniting businessmen and officials to consolidate their political power. Psychologists even argue that "people desire power not to be a master over others, but to be master of their own domain, to control their own fate," because "almost everyone in a modern organization is controlled by some, and only top managers are free from control. Therefore, people from all levels of an organization experience some lack of autonomy and therefore some desire for power" (Lammers et al. 2016, p. 498). The case of Lu Enguang exemplifies office purchase motivated by power hunger. Lu bribed many leaders to become an official because he was obsessed with controlling others, rather than with taking bribes from them.[27] Ordinary cadres, who do not expect to control enormous power, may buy offices for career advancement along the government ranks. Promotion may not substantially increase their power, but it can boost their salary and social status.

Finally, a strong preference for joining the government or becoming an employee of the state is embedded in Chinese culture. According to Xinhua News Agency, the ratio of applicants to posts in the national civil servant examination is around 70:1.[28] Shangdong province is a classic example; most of the young people whom I interviewed there considered being a state employee – including a public school teacher, a doctor in a public hospital, an SOE employee, and a civil servant – the ideal job. Civil servant posts are preferred. People favor these occupations because of their stability, their high societal status, and the potential benefits deriving from that status, including advantages in the marriage market.[29] These views echo the widespread purchasing of posts in hospitals, schools, and SOEs and even the purchasing of entrance to colleges and schools at the grassroots level.

---

26 See https://news.sina.cn/gn/2016-06-12/detail-ifxszfak3597066.d.html.

27 CCDI documentary www.youtube.com/watch?v=Zg3zp-MiCsc.

28 See www.news.cn/politics/2023-01/08/c_1129264303.htm.

29 Interview conducted in September 2023.

4.5 The Office-Selling Order

Once buying and selling offices become prevalent, an alternative elite mobility order may be established, generating peer pressure that draws more individuals into personnel corruption. Individuals who do not follow this norm may face discrimination in political selection. Primitive bribery may develop into evolved bribery and even office-selling syndicates and oligarchical power bases. As more officials follow suit, sporadic office purchases can grow into a market for public posts, which can expand both from the top down and the bottom up, as well as across administrative and geographical boundaries. Only strong political will to curb such personnel corruption can shatter this order.

In general, personnel corruption has roots in both the demand and supply sides. It is embedded in Chinese culture, which values official posts, and sustained by the authoritarian political system, which concentrates power and relies on power to secure wealth and more power. Besides the simplest motivations of financial and political greed and opportunism, structural flaws allow office-selling to occur. Investigating personnel corruption is difficult by institutional design. Businessmen are willing to "invest" in candidates by bribing senior officials on their behalf. Most significantly, the opaque and age-limited nature of the cadre-promotion process encourages bribery as a means of moving ahead. Young civil servants face a system in which they must be promoted as high and as quickly as possible to avoid being seen as "too old"; in which competition for entry-level positions is already immense; and in which the actual requirements for moving forward are not always clear. Junior officials actively look for senior mentors who can act as useful connections to move their careers along, and the most immediate and simplest way to build these connections is bribery.

5 Purchase versus Performance and Patronage: A Third Paradigm?

Money can play a significant role in political competition in China. However, to answer the question raised at the beginning (i.e., to what extent can the influence of money alter the competitive dynamics of political selection that scholarly explanations suggest?), we should concretely explore how rent seeking is balanced with performance and patronage in political selection and whether and when rent seeking takes precedence over or even overrides performance and patronage. Such scenarios would especially support the adoption of a third purchase paradigm to provide distinct explanations of political selection and how bribery constitutes a de facto separate path for cadres' advancement in China. Hence, what a leader seeks from their subordinates and how the leader prioritizes those goals are crucial. As discussed in Section 1, in the performance paradigm, leaders mainly look for subordinates' delivery of observable growth, which is often believed to reflect competence; in the patronage paradigm, leaders are most concerned with subordinates' personal ties, and ultimately, their loyalty. The focus on competence and loyalty originates from the literature arguing that autocratic leaders often face a tradeoff between loyalty and competence when selecting advisors and subordinates. Competent subordinates are better able to plot betrayal and threaten the ruler's power, while loyal subordinates lack the competence needed to effectively manage the state and maintain the regime's stability. Paranoid rulers may prefer less competent but more loyal advisors for power security (Wintrobe 1998; Egorov & Sonin 2011).

Although inspiring, studies of this tradeoff overlook other possible factors affecting elites' promotion and alternative political selection models in authoritarian regimes.[30] Moreover, the framework was originally proposed as the *dictator*'s dilemma of political selection at the very top of the state hierarchy. Do subnational leaders, who presumably have less stake in the regime, face the same dilemma when making personnel decisions? Research on China has already shown that competence and loyalty can be differently prioritized at different levels or in places with different socioeconomic conditions (e.g., Zuo 2015; Landry, Lü, & Duan 2018; Yan & Yuan 2020). Neither are all officials equally incentivized by the prospect of promotion, given the age constraints involved (Manion 2023). Laggards in promotion may have more incentives to accept and solicit bribes when selecting subordinates, as shown in Section 4.

Thus, in this section, I reexamine the office-selling cases in my datasets by focusing on the relationship between bribery and performance and patronage. I consider how leaders balance personal ties (i.e., loyalty), competence, and money during personnel decision-making and particularly try to identify circumstances where rent seeking is prioritized as direct evidence of bribery being a de facto third path to power. In cases where capital is used to build relationships, I compare personal ties based on money with those based on common experiences, the traditional proxy for loyalty in studies of Chinese elite politics. I argue that if these two kinds of personal ties diverge, promotions obtained through bribery should be distinguished from those based on patronage in the traditional sense.

5.1 Purchase and Patronage

Patronage is based on personal ties, through which the patron fundamentally wants the clients' loyalty. However, loyalty has been poorly defined in the literature.

[30] Emerging studies start to study physical appearance of politicians in authoritarian regimes (e.g., Wong & Zeng 2017; Jiang & Yang 2024; Wang, Li, & Praino 2024) but use perceived competence and loyalty as the main criteria to judge outlook.

Loyalty has many layers of meaning (Smith 2020). Fletcher (1993) differentiated between a minimalist understanding of loyalty – do not betray me – and a maximalist interpretation – become united with me. Egorov and Sonin (2011) take the minimalist reading, in which "loyalty" basically means failing to betray a dictator or commit treason. However, in research and practice, loyalty usually means more than simply non-betrayal. For instance, Souryal and McKay (1996) argue that "the ideal of loyalty has its *roots* in the virtue of sympathy, which is at the foundation of all human experience" (p. 44). Benzel (2024) defines loyalty as "a strong feeling of support or allegiance to another person or group of persons, an ideal, a duty, or a cause" (p. XIX). Hence, loyalty has affective components, such as sympathy, support, trust, and a sense of belonging, and even some moral components. These affect facets can strengthen "non-betrayal," therefore, authoritarian leaders would also care.

Additionally, the political selection literature focuses on personal loyalty, as distinct from modern loyalty. According to Weber (2013), a decisive component of modern loyalty "is that, in the pure type, it does not establish a relationship to a *person*, like the vassal's or the disciple's faith in feudal or patrimonial relations of authority . . ., modern loyalty is devoted to impersonal and functional purposes" (p. 199). The term "organizational loyalty" offers a clearer contrast with personal loyalty, which is directed toward an individual or a community rather than a faceless institution (Shih 2004, p. 4). Personal loyalty to a superior tends to involve deference, obedience, and subordination to an individual and may involve "selling out" (Souryal & McKay 1996), such as abandoning one's principles and judgments. This partially explains why Egorov and Sonin (2011) assume a pure tradeoff between competence and loyalty and that loyalty means incompetence.

5.1.1 Four Types of Relationships between Loyalty and Bribery

A close examination of office-selling cases helps us understand how leaders consider loyalty during political selection and its relationship with bribery. I distinguish four types of relationships between loyalty and bribery: (1) loyalty trumps monetary gains; that is, leaders forgo less trustworthy candidates with larger bribes to promote individuals who offer smaller bribes but are more trustworthy; (2) loyalty via bribery, that is, the consistent use of bribery to signal loyalty and cultivate ties with one's superior; (3) monetary gains on top of loyalty, that is, a leader sells positions at an equal price to every office buyer or the highest "bidder" with which they are familiar; and (4) bribery devoid of loyalty, that is, promotions are predominantly based on bribery, with little consideration of loyalty. The importance of loyalty to promotion decreases from types 1 to 4, while the influence of bribery increases. I elaborate on these four types next.

First, loyalty trumps monetary gains. This relationship may help validate the patronage paradigm, where personal ties and loyalty are a leader's primary concerns in political selection. For instance, in the Heilongjiang office-selling chain, an individual known for their devoted allegiance could secure the position of a county Party secretary role for the relatively modest sum of RMB100,000. Others could only attain the second-highest position, that of county governor, at a significantly higher cost, RMB300,000 (Zhu 2008). As this case shows, even for leaders who have engaged in office-selling, the desire to ensure subordinates' compliance can override financial temptations. The cost of securing promotions and appointments can be conditional on the personal relationships between superiors and their subordinates. Those perceived as loyal and supportive of their superiors' directives may find career advancement opportunities at more affordable rates than those lacking such close ties. The oligarchical power bases of Ling Jihua and Zhou Yongkang also indicate that loyalty, or at least fairly strong preexisting personal ties, are an important prerequisite for officials to join the "high-end corruption club." Members of Ling Jihua's Xishan Society were primarily townsmen of Shanxi province, providing them with a basis for mutual trust. In Zhou Yongkang's corrupt empire, several key players, such as Guo Yongxiang and Jiang Jiemin, were his long-time trusted followers. The prerequisite for loyalty also meets the need for political power defense in oligarchical power bases.

However, personal ties do not create themselves and loyalty is private information. This gives rise to the second type of relationship between loyalty and bribery: namely, loyalty via bribery. In this case, subordinates consistently bribe a superior to get close to them and signal loyalty. As argued by Feng, Weng, and Zhang (2024), leaders who prioritize loyalty may screen candidates carefully with costly tests to rule out untrustworthy ones. Sizable monetary payments, although less bloody and flamboyant than political purges, campaigns, and executions (e.g., Shih 2008; Qian & Bai 2024), can still be considered a kind of credible sacrifice according to signaling theory (e.g., Bird & Smith 2005). For example, as mentioned in Section 2, Wang Like looked for every opportunity to get close to Sun Lijun by continuously bribing Sun for several years, with bribes totaling RMB90 million, and became trusted by Sun, who in return helped with several of his promotions. Similar practices also exist at lower administrative levels. In Dataset B, not only were public holidays the most popular occasions for office buyers to pay off their superiors, but many individuals took several holidays in a row to get close to their leaders. For example, in nearly 2,500 bribery exchanges in the dataset, more than 25% of the office buyers bribed the office sellers multiple times. Among them, more than twenty individuals paid twenty times or more, and more than fifty paid ten times or more. Such consecutive payoffs strongly indicate the use of money to cultivate closer ties in the hope of receiving long-term patronage, rather than a single promotion. In one case, a public hospital doctor visited his hospital head every Spring Festival between 1994 and 2017 and sent "red packets" to him thirty-nine times, totaling RMB525,000. He was promoted to deputy head of the hospital and received other help from the head. In the evolved bribery case of Wang Gengdong discussed in Section 3, the office buyer was trusted by Wang to commit corrupt acts.

In the third type, "monetary gains on top of loyalty," loyalty or a close personal tie is at most a precondition; what mainly affects promotion is money. We can infer this type from cases in which a leader sold similar positions to a few direct subordinates at similar or even fixed prices. In Dataset B, Xie Shousheng took bribes from several cadres to help with their promotions while serving as head of a prefectural health bureau in Fujian province. Six of his subordinates in the public health system paid him the same price of RMB20,000 and received one-level-up promotions in township hospitals, such as from vice-director to director of a department. In another case, Zhang Yujiang took advantage of his power as deputy mayor and Party committee member of a municipality of Xinjiang, helping six subordinates with promotions. Each of the six officials was at the division level (*chu*), visited Zhang during holidays over four years, and sent him a total of RMB50,000. In both examples, the office buyers were subordinates of and known to the office sellers. Especially in Zhang's case, as discussed previously, paying continuously was a way to demonstrate loyalty to one's leader. However, the fact that the same price was charged implies either that every office buyer was assumed to be equally loyal by the superior or that, once a certain level of connection is established, loyalty is no longer crucial to personnel selection. Therefore, paying a bribe resembles buying a permit to a higher position, or going the "extra mile" to set oneself apart. Bribery in this situation is almost the only way to earn a promotion on top of loyalty.

The fourth type is "bribery devoid of loyalty," in which personnel selection is influenced primarily by bribery, with little consideration of loyalty. In my datasets, we can infer the existence of this type primarily from grassroots personnel corruption involving low-entrance jobs and school admissions. In these cases, many bribers were not direct subordinates of the bribees but rather outsiders to the bribees' systems, who were only introduced to them by middlemen. Office buyers' low frequency of visits to office sellers (e.g., only once), in contrast with the previous type, also reflects the limited cultivation of personal ties by the bribers and the weak personal ties between the two sides. For example, in Dataset B, Lian Wei, Party secretary and director of a county-level housing and urban–rural development bureau took bribes (approximately RMB50,000 per post) from several government outsiders, including small business owners and laid off SOE workers, to help their children get jobs in state-owned plants under his bureau. Similarly, Wu Gang, a district-level director of an education bureau in Anhui province, took bribes from different people to arrange for their children to be teachers in primary schools in his district.

Bribery devoid of loyalty may also happen in leadership positions. For instance, Cui Zongxing, a county DOO head discussed in Section 3, sold more than eighty-eight positions to sixty-seven people. Among the thirty-five cadres who sought promotions for township leadership positions, most paid similar prices, of around RMB5,000, and swiftly received their desired posts. The quantity of sales and the speed of delivery indicate the commercialization of promotion in this case, distinguishing it from office-selling by Xie and Zhang in the third type, "bribery on top of loyalty." Additionally, the office buyers here were not Cui's direct subordinates in the organization system and lacked strong preexisting personal ties with him, again in contrast with the cases of Xie and Zhang. We cannot assume that Cui was equally familiar with thirty-five cadres or perceived them as equally loyal. It is more likely that financial gains overrode other concerns.

In general, this investigation shows that, first, many leaders do prioritize loyalty or at least set a certain level of personal connection as a prerequisite in subordinate selection. Second, however, capital can pave the way for career advancement in addition to or separately from connections in several circumstances. Third and equally important, loyalty, a quality that superiors look for in candidates, is candidates' private information; superiors can only judge perceived loyalty, which can result from candidates' active building of stronger personal ties, including through financial means.

5.1.2 Personal Ties in Office Purchase versus Clientelist Ties in Factions

However, personal ties in office purchase and clientelist ties in factions, or factional ties, the classic synonym for or proxy of patronage or loyalty in research on Chinese political elites, have nuances. Although Nathan (1973, p. 37) in his seminal article on CCP's factionalism argues that two-person clientelist ties, as the foundation of factions, involve a "constant exchange of gifts and services" (p. 37), he does not explicitly equate this exchange to corruption.

Even more importantly, factional ties tend to emerge from common experiences eliciting affective relationships, such as serving in the same regiment during wartime or having a shared hometown, school, or workplace (e.g., Whitson & Huang 1973; Pye 1981; Lieberthal & Oksenberg 1988; Li 2001; Shih, Adolph, & Liu 2012;Yang, Xu & Tao 2014; Keller 2016; Meyer, Shih, & Lee 2016; Doyon & Keller 2020; Wiebe 2020; Yan & Yuan 2020). Thus, two-person clientelist ties based on common experience can develop into group loyalty among multiple members sharing the same experience. The bedrock idea of group loyalty is membership of a group that competes with other groups (Fletcher 1993). Being a member places one within a network of connections with fellow members and the organization's leadership, creating a sense of belonging and identity (Fletcher 1993). Group insiders' membership, although informal, establishes a network in which for them to connect and form tiers of ties with individual leaders to mobilize "for the purpose of engaging in politics," forming a faction (Nathan 1973, p. 37). Members remain bonded by their factional relationships even after political engagement or receiving a promotion. Among Chinese elites, factional membership identity is manifested in coalitions popularly recognized by scholars and the public, such as "princelings" (offspring of high-ranking officials), the "Shanghai gang" (leaders who advanced their political careers in Shanghai when Jiang was Party chief there in the 1980s), and *tuanpai* (leaders who were former Chinese CYL officials) (Li 2012).

In contrast, money is the fundamental glue binding the participants of office sales together. This does not mean that office sellers and buyers lack informal connections, such as the same birthplaces, or professional and educational connections. Nonetheless, those commonalities are only stepping stones to get closer to a leader so that visiting and giving money are less awkward and abrupt. As Engvall (2015) argues regarding office-selling in the post-Soviet states, informal connections still matter, but they primarily mediate "access to the 'investment market,'" at the heart of which a monetary logic operates (p. 35). Thus, loyalty built via bribery, if any, focuses on personal relationships with the leader and stays at the personal level with the office seller, especially in cases of primitive and evolved bribery. Even in office-selling syndicates, office buyers do not necessarily know each other or consider themselves in alliance.

Oligarchical power bases resemble traditional factions most in terms of membership identity and potential engagement in politics, as exemplified by Ling's Society or Zhou's gangs. However, the membership identity of power base insiders can be murky, and the mechanisms for maintaining group loyalty in such power bases often involve a mix of benefits, perks, mutual hostage, and blackmail between members, rather than interpersonal trust or friendship, as commonly assumed in factionalism (Nathan 1973; Darden 2001; Keller 2016). As observed by Rithmire and Chen (2021) in "mafia-like business systems in China" (p. 1048), the superficial closeness between economic elites and political elites in some circumstances signals not mutual trust or simple patron–client relationships but mutual endangerment. The "logic is to implicate and threaten and typically entails implicating as many factions and families as possible" into illicit dealings "to widen the net of the system's protection" (2021). Underlying mutual endangerment is the fear of others' defection and "acrimony," by which participants hold "information about corrupt dealings that could potentially be used to discredit" and incriminate others (p. 1047). Thus, "collaboration" maintained in this way cannot be "abrogated by either member at will," as in normal clientelist ties (Nathan 1973, p. 37). Ironically, loyalty coerced in such connections may crumble in the face of anticorruption campaigns, which may trigger participants to betray each other (Feng, Weng, & Zhang 2024).

Another subtle difference between personal ties in buying and selling offices and factions lies in the well-understood (albeit often implicitly) "rights and obligations between the partners" (Nathan 1973, p. 37). Besides the avoidance of betrayal, personal loyalty in authoritarian politics means that subordinates are expected to actively "make their superiors look good, especially when they do not" (Souryal & McKay 1996, p. 46). In China, when a factional patron comes under attack, they can mobilize their followers to counterattack. Followers protect a patron in the expectation of large payoffs, such as promotion to the upper echelons of the regime (Shih, Adolph, & Liu 2012). Personal loyalty also requires a subordinate to make sacrifices, such as setting aside significant personal interests or enduring the social cost of being scorned by others (Souryal & McKay 1996; Shih 2008). These more complex motives, rights, and obligations may not exist between superiors and subordinates who are bound together through buying and selling offices, except in oligarchical power bases that focus on gaining power and defending wealth. In office-selling cases devoid of loyalty, leaders sell positions to office buyers mainly for monetary profits, probably without more sophisticated expectations or the possibility of more mobilization. For example, in grassroots personnel corruption, buyers are positioned too far below office sellers to provide them with meaningful support in power struggles. When DOO heads sell positions, although office buyers may receive more important posts, the DOO in practice does not have direct leadership over those posts, which could limit the opportunity and incentive for office buyers to make DOO heads look good. Therefore, these situations, similar to office sales in premodern Britain (Allen 2005), do not involve strong expectations of personal loyalty for the office sellers or buyers, making money the main instrument leveraged for promotion. I summarize the Section 5.1 in Table 6, which uses a modified checklist of Nathan's (1973) "hallmarks" of clientelist ties of factions as a reference baseline for comparison with the personal ties in the four types of sale of offices.

Therefore, bribery in office purchase has dual functions – pure capital investment and personal tie cultivation. Despite some overlapping characteristics, as demonstrated in Table 6, personal ties based on money are largely distinct from factional ties based on common experiences. They have diverse mechanisms for maintaining loyalty or collaboration between members, political agendas, and organizational structures. Table 6 also indicates that the weights of bribery's two functions vary in specific cases. Generally, the level of personal tie cultivation is lowest for primitive bribery, followed by office-selling syndicates and evolved bribery. Among these three types, office-selling syndicates involve the strongest rent-seeking incentives, where rent seeking is sometimes the primary goal. Oligarchical power bases are the most similar to traditionally discussed factions. However, their manipulative internal interpersonal relations, ambiguous group identity, and lack of exit mechanism distinguish such power bases from regular factions.

5.2 Purchase and Performance

If loyalty and competence have a tradeoff relationship, how about bribery and performance? In Egorov and Sonin's (2011) framework, competent means "cunning": Being able to conceal ulterior intentions and unravel complex situations, such as defection plots. In Chinese politics, as mentioned previously, competence is largely equated to or measured by leaders' economic performance and other visible political achievements or merits, such as higher education attainment.

Contrasting the inherent intricate relationship between loyalty and bribery, bribery is often thought to be conducted by candidates with poor performance, incompetent governance, or low merit. Thus, is office buyers' meritocracy completely irrelevant to promotion decisions when offices are bought? The relationship is less simple. I summarize four kinds of situations: (1) "Monetary gains over performance": Candidates' administrative performance is ignored in personnel decisions, and bribers may be promoted despite their obviously low performance record. (2) "Performance falsified for promotion": Candidates' performance is ostensibly considered, with office buyers giving bribes for attractive performance indicators, such as falsified track records or good evaluation results, to assist their promotions. (3) "Merit over bribes": The superior considers office buyers' eligibility in terms of merit when making promotion decisions, and promotion requests may be rejected if candidates are found to be ineligible. (4) "Forced bribery by competent officials": Competent officials give bribes to obtain promotions under the peer pressure of buying offices.

Table 6 Comparison between factional ties and personal ties in four types of office purchase

Clientelist ties in factions	**Personal ties in primitive bribery**	**Personal ties in evolved bribery**	**Personal ties in office-selling syndicates**	**Personal ties in oligarchical power bases**
(1) Relationship between two people as the foundation	Same as clientelist ties in factions: In the context of office purchase, the two people are the office seller (the leader) and the office buyer (the subordinate)			
(2) Relationship especially selected for cultivation by the members from their total social networks	Same as clientelist ties in factions for office buyers, but the office sellers may or may not select buyers			Similar to factional ties, both sides of office purchase are careful when selecting partners
(3) Cultivated essentially by the constant exchange of gifts or services	One-time exchange of bribes in most cases, sometimes multiple times of exchanges	Constant transfer of benefits and services in most cases	One-time exchange of bribes in most cases; sometimes multiple exchanges	Constant transfer of benefits and services in most cases
(4) Unequal wealth and power between the leader and the subordinate	Same as clientelist ties in factions: unequal wealth and power between office buyers and sellers			
(5) Tie sets up well-understood rights	Clear and narrow rights and	Well-understood and evolving rights and	Generally well-understood and	Most similar to rights and obligations

Table 6 (cont.)

Clientelist ties in factions	Personal ties in primitive bribery	Personal ties in evolved bribery	Personal ties in office-selling syndicates	Personal ties in oligarchical power bases
and obligations between partners, for example, the leader helps the subordinate with promotion; the subordinate supports the leader in conflicts	obligations, for example, leader helps subordinate with promotions	obligations, for example, besides promotion, subordinate helps leader with corrupt dealings	narrow rights and obligations, for example, leader helps subordinate with promotions	involved in factional ties, for example, subordinate helps leader defend political power and wealth
(6) Can be abrogated by either member at will	Same, for example, office sellers may return bribes to office buyers if favor is not delivered	Same, for example, office sellers may not deliver the purchased favor	Same, for example, office sellers may return bribes or make alternative arrangements for office buyers as they deem appropriate	Not easy to abrogate at will due to mutual endangerment
(7) Either member free to establish other simultaneous ties	Same, not exclusive, although the office seller in this type usually only engages in selling offices once or twice	Same as in primitive bribery	Same, not exclusive	Same, not exclusive

(8) Internal relations usually feature interpersonal trust, often developed from common experiences	Internal relations feature a certain level of interpersonal trust to sustain monetary exchange	Internal relations feature higher interpersonal trust than that of primitive bribery to sustain transfer of benefits	Similar to primitive bribery	Internal relations combine interpersonal trust and interpersonal threat to maintain loyalty
(9) Leader mobilizes layers of clientelist ties to engage in politics	Only one layer of personal ties; no engagement in politics in most cases.	Same as primitive bribery	Multiple layers of personal ties can exist in office-selling chains, usually with no engagement in politics	Same as clientelist ties in factions
(10) Potential to develop group loyalty/ membership identity	No group	No group	Office buyers may not know each other or form alliances	Group membership is murky

Note: (1) to (7) are cited from Nathan (1973) with slight rephrasing. Other points are added to the list based on the previous comparisons.

In the first situation, formal criteria for evaluating performance and competence, such as the candidates' educational attainment, track record, and integrity, which are often reputedly screened during political selection, are ignored. For example, Zheng Wentong, a county-level DOO head in Dataset B, helped Xu's promotion. Xu did not manage well the Party-building work for which he was responsible and ranked last in the annual assessment. In 2013, Xu went to Zheng's office under the pretext of reporting work and gave him RMB10,000 in cash as a New Year's gift. Afterward, Xu was only orally criticized for his poor performance in a countywide announcement by the county committee. Half a year later, he was promoted to township deputy Party secretary and mayor. In the public health sector, a public hospital doctor was ranked at the bottom in a department directors' evaluation at the end of 2014 and had to participate in an extra round of competition to continue as a department director. This doctor gave Du, the leader of the hospital and public health authority of the prefecture, a shopping card worth RMB10,000 at New Year in 2015. Du intervened to ensure that the assessor gave the doctor the highest score, enabling him to continue serving as department director. In these cases, the office buyers were promoted or they successfully retained their positions despite their poor performance being publicly known, directly contradicting the performance paradigm. Competence was at best secondary to the bribes given.

In the second situation, merit criteria were nominally pursued, while office buyers' glamorous portfolios were fabricated or bought. A representative case is that of Lu Enguang, mentioned multiple times previously. He was a former member of the Ministry of Justice's leading Party group. The CCDI called him a "five fake" cadre because he was found to have fabricated personal records of age, family, educational background, work history, and CCP membership documents and employed financial resources, personal connections, and lobbying tactics to acquire official posts and honorary titles to progress from a private business owner to a vice-ministerial-level official.[31] In the office-selling syndicate of a county Party secretary discussed in Section 3, Liu Chunmao accepted RMB50,000 from Pan, the director of Shangnan county's Commerce and Trade Bureau (CTB), to help the CTB obtain a better ranking across the entire city. Such cases are more deceptive than those in the first situation and meritocracy is at least considered at face value. Bribery helps to "dress up" office buyers as qualified candidates, making their promotion seem legitimate.

In the third situation, "merit over bribes," office sellers appear to consider candidates' merit more seriously than in the previous two situations. Highly

[31] See www.thestandard.com.hk/breaking-news/section/2/89934/Justice-official-expelled-from-CPC-for-faking-resume-and-bribery.

unsuitable individuals may fail to receive the positions requested, despite sending bribes. For example, in Liu Chunmao's office-selling syndicate, one office buyer, Zhao, wanted to be promoted to town mayor. However, Liu thought that Zhao's experience was too limited to make him a good fit for town mayor and thus instructed the county DOO head to arrange for Zhao to serve as chairman of the township people's congress. One may suspect that "insufficient experience" is only an excuse for superiors to solicit more money from their subordinates, but this doubt does not seem to hold, at least in some cases. For instance, in Fu Zhanwen's primitive bribery case (Section 3), the size of the bribe was not the primary concern of Fu's leader, as he returned half of the money to Fu after giving him a lateral transfer instead of a headship. Xue Linchao, former head of a district public security bureau in Henan province, repeatedly claimed in court that several of the officials he had promoted were competent and popular with their colleagues, and that they had given him money as a gratuity for the promotions. Several court judgments in Dataset B likewise mentioned superiors' consideration of candidates' eligibility in personnel decisions while accepting their money.

The last situation involves competent officials paying bribes due to peer pressure, as competent officials do not benefit from staying out of the corrupt networks. Failing to follow the norm could put them at risk of being replaced by those willing to actively purchase positions. Thus, competent cadres may feel compelled to acquiesce to the informal rules and participate. For instance, in the Heilongjiang office-selling chain, a capable young female cadre was promoted by Han Guizhi and chose to express her gratitude financially, as recommended by her colleagues, by sending Han RMB300,000 (Zhu 2008).

Overall, in the first two situations, bribery greatly precedes performance or candidates' competence in political selection. In the last situation, bribery also plays a crucial role in securing promotion opportunities for qualified candidates. Only in the third situation does money have little effect on the prerequisite of candidates' performance. Considering all four situations, (1) we cannot simply conclude that only incompetent officials choose to buy promotions; however, (2) capital support can greatly assist candidates who originally appear ineligible or less competitive by formal promotion standards. According to one former official, "As long as money is sufficient, everything is not a problem"; some officials even believe that their failure to send money to leaders prevents them from obtaining promotions.[32] Thus, performance, whose importance to political selection is often questioned by researchers, may be placed even lower under the influence of money.

[32] See www.ordoslz.gov.cn/single/2018/04/12/190305115250511835 85-18083015510919453828 .html?t=1665295703938.

5.3 Mapping Promotion in a Tripartite Framework

Purchase is a viable third dimension, along with patronage and performance, of a framework for reimagining political selection in China. In some cases, it directly influences personnel decisions; in others, money exerts an indirect influence through patronage or performance by contributing to the cultivation of personal ties or falsification of credentials. Therefore, reimagining promotion as occurring in a tripartite context in which the three paradigms make weighted contributions is reasonable. Ideally, if we knew the weight of each dimension in all the personnel decisions, we could infer the dominant model of political selection in China and its dynamics, such as how multiple models compete and coexist over time.

I map office purchase cases with complete information in Dataset B to the framework. Though such cases are few, especially for certain types, the visualization can still give us a taste of what the tripartite framework can illuminate about political selection. I innovatively utilize details in the court judgments to measure the three dimensions, using proxies substantiated by insights from previous in-depth case studies. The weight of purchase is measured by the size of bribes in each case. The weight of performance is proxied by office buyers' educational attainment, following common practice when other standardized capability measures are missing (e.g., Jia 2022). Patronage measurement is a weighted sum of three indices signaling personal ties. The baseline index is my coding of bribe forms, "transfer of benefits" versus "direct monetary payment" (Section 3), as the former involves stronger personal ties than the latter. This is supplemented by additional information on tie cultivation gleaned from court judgments, as follows. (1) The number of times a briber visited a bribee or paid money to them; larger numbers indicate more relationship-building and potentially stronger ties. (2) Whether a briber paid bribes both before and after receiving favors; an answer of "yes" denotes more relationship building. I assign weights of 0.36, 0.32, and 0.32, respectively, to the three indices.[33] Figure 22(a) visualizes the distribution of different types of office purchase in the tripartite space, and its rotatable version is accessible in the online version of this Element. Figure 22(b) plots the cases across 2D planes of every pairwise dimension for each type. The three dimensions are scaled to 1 for easy comparison.

Primitive bribery (blue circle) and office-selling syndicates (purple diamond) are generally lower in the cube than evolved bribery (green triangle) and oligarchical power bases (red square), because their baseline patronage score is lower. Many primitive bribery cases are also distributed along the lower bound of the

[33] Weights mainly affect the visualization, not the statistical significance of the findings.

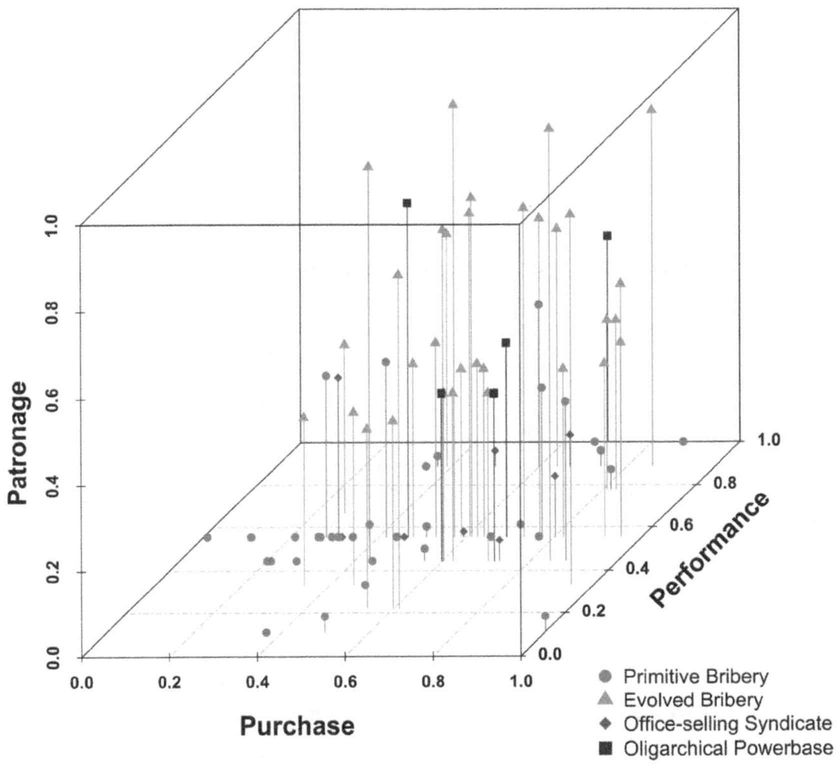

Figure 22a Mapping office purchase cases to the tripartite framework by type. Rotatable version of this figure is available to view online at www.cambridge.org/Zhu

purchase axis, indicating small to medium-sized amounts of capital involved, whereas other types of bribery rely on larger amounts of capital, indicating the importance of money to promotions. Regressions show especially large differences between the amounts involved in primitive bribery and evolved bribery.[34] Additionally, numerous evolved bribery cases, oligarchical power bases, and even office-selling syndicates are found toward the upper-right corner of the cube, demonstrating a high synergy of purchase, performance, and patronage. Bribery also contributes significantly to the patronage dimension in several cases. As explained previously regarding the measurement of patronage, bar heights above 0.36 for evolved bribery and oligarchical power bases and bars above the bottom for primitive bribery and office-selling syndicates are the result of personal tie cultivation assisted by money, such as multiple visits with payoffs. The synergy of the three dimensions shows that political selection is not necessarily

[34] The results are available upon request.

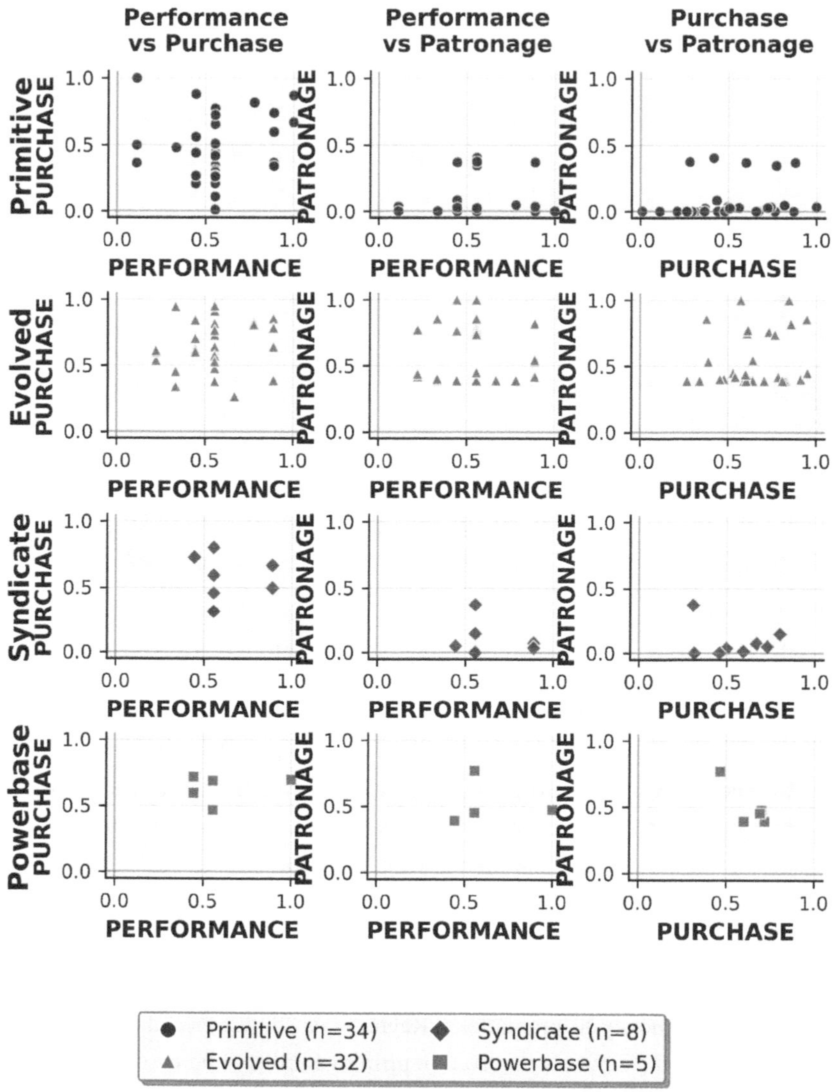

Figure 22b Pairwise 2D version

subject to a tradeoff between competence and loyalty but the result of a deep mixture of three selection logics: performance represents the basic condition for promotion, while stronger personal ties are crucial and often monetarily costly.

5.4 Why Use a Tripartite Framework?

If more promotion cases were mapped to the tripartite space in Figure 22, promotions based on different combinations of political selection logics would be likely to form various large and small clusters. The distribution of the clusters in the 3D space can reflect how multiple states coexist and potentially compete for dominance. Thus, the tripartite framework of political selection can shed light on the previously overlooked logic of elite politics and even state-building in authoritarian regimes. For instance, examining the rampant office sales in post-Soviet Eurasian states, Engvall (2015) advises scholars to "roll back the analysis to the step before Max Weber's modern institutionalized state" and to first question "how the state is constituted" (p. 26). He conceptualizes the functioning of these states as investments in a market, which is neither "the rule-governed and impersonal administrative structure found in modern states" nor "personalistic rule," because "money rather than parochial ties are the dominant feature of political and administrative organization" (p. 28). While it would be an exaggeration to describe the Chinese administrative matrix as "an investment market," the cases of primitive bribery clustered at the bottom of Figure 22(a) illustrate an emerging primitive "investment market state" with accessible prices, where humble capital drives political selection.

Along with recognizing the potential influence of money in elite mobility, it is important to note that the distinction between grand and petty corruption often drawn in the literature may overlook the similar investment dynamics that shape state behaviors at all levels. Grand and petty corruption may be connected in a reciprocal market, and petty corruption, which ordinary citizens can more easily experience and observe, may reflect grand corruption. Ultimately, what remains are offices that offer varying prospects for generating revenue (Engvall 2015).

Moreover, taking personal ties based on bribery seriously could help differentiate the "taxonomy of factions" in Chinese elite politics. Miller (2015) remarks that one issue rarely addressed "is the taxonomy of political associations that are lumped together under the rubric of 'factions'" (p. 6). However, "China's contemporary political ecology is populated by diverse species of groups whose bases differ, whose nature and strength of connections vary, and whose links into national politics are often obscure" (2015). Hence, from another perspective, office-selling syndicates and oligarchical power base identified in this Element could be considered as new "species" under the large family of "factions," distinct from the traditional factions based on common experiences discussed in the literature. As Nathan and Tsai (1995) argue:

> If we know on what basis members associate with one another we can understand something about how highly committed they are, what their goals and interests are, what rewards they require from the leadership, and what sacrifices the leaders can ask from them. This in turn helps us predict whether the group is capable of postponing gratification of its members in pursuit of long-term strategies, whether it can use violence, and whether it can outlast the lives of its members. (p. 169)

The "new species" and traditional factions, due to their different bases, act differently in many of the those respects. Office-selling syndicates, with their business orientation, have little political agenda. Oligarchical power bases most closely resemble traditional factions and may engage in political struggles to defend the ruling oligarchs' political power. However, their positions in the elite power configuration relative to traditional factions and their strong desire to defend their wealth could greatly influence their policymaking and implementation. They may instrumentalize their policy influences to serve power bases narrowly, as exemplified by Zhou Yongkang's capitalizing on the central authorities' fear of public unrest (Wang & Minzner 2015). Their engagement in power competition and hollowing out state coffers will eventually threaten the central authorities. A supreme leader who prefers to centralize power will be most sensitive to oligarchical power bases.

6 Restart the Party: How Central Authorities Combat Personnel Corruption

Based on case studies of the Heilongjiang office-selling chain, I previously argued that the diffusion of selling offices can result in the privatization of public power and deinstitutionalization of meritocracy, a theoretical pillar of the modern state (Zhu 2008). These outcomes still hold in most circumstances in this Element's systematic examination of the sale of offices. Does this mean that buying and selling offices necessarily undermine regime resilience? What are the other implications of extensive personnel corruption?

6.1 Implications of Buying and Selling Offices

Lawrence Zhang (2022) studies the purchase of official appointments in Qing China as an officially legitimate means to acquire promotions as an alternative to examinations. Zhang argues that this pathway provided more opportunities for elite mobility and made the "purchase class" feel more tied to the regime, as they "literally invested money into this enterprise and expected something in return" (p. 24). Although purchasing offices is illegal in contemporary China, does office buyers' capital investment also strengthen or at least maintain their attachment to the regime? To some extent, the answer is yes, because cadres who purchase promotions will only benefit, politically or economically, from the survival and even prosperity of the Party-state. In this respect, the relationship between purchasing offices and regime survival is parallel to that between "access money" and fast economic growth in China (Ang 2020). Therefore, the prospect of career advancement created by capital, although at odds with formal institutions, may informally tie political elites to the regime.

However, selling offices may also gradually lead to regime decay. It inflates economic corruption because capital investment in power naturally seeks monetary returns. In fact, there are several reasons to expect a negative correlation between personnel corruption and economic development. For instance, Sun (2004) proposes that office-selling tends to be more severe in less economically developed areas because few lucrative corruption opportunities exist in those localities. Guardado (2018), based on her hand-collected dataset of the sale of colonial provincial governorships by the Spanish Crown in seventeenth- and eighteenth-century Peru, argues that office-selling in colonies resulted in the negative selection of officials and long-term negative impacts on local socioeconomic development. Indeed, Section 5.2 shows that candidates' competence can be more easily compromised if appointments and promotions are put up for sale, although competent individuals may also choose to buy promotions. Signaling an alternative causal mechanism between personnel corruption and poor socioeconomic performance, the Heilongjiang case shows that office-selling chains can undermine economic development by diverting funds from business investment to the purchase of offices (Zhu 2008).

Therefore, I statistically test the relationship between personnel corruption and the local economy by combining Dataset B and the replication data from Landry, Lü, & Duan (2018). I use the number of ongoing office-selling cases and the number of investigated cases by year and province to measure the severity of buying and selling offices in Dataset B, and I use the number of office-selling syndicates to examine this subtype's relationship with economic development.[35] I use local nighttime light brightness as the dependent variable, as it is increasingly considered a more reliable measure of economic prosperity than GDP, and many of the values of common economic growth indicators, such as GDP and fiscal revenue, are missing at the prefecture and county levels (Wallace 2016). I control local populations and local leaders' ages, which could affect local economic growth (Guo 2009). More details of the measures are provided in online Appendix B. Results of OLS regressions with fixed effects are presented in Table 7.

In Models 1–4 (Table 7), the two measures of personnel corruption are generally negatively correlated with nighttime light brightness at the prefecture and county levels. Intuitively, this result suggests a difficult situation where ongoing office-selling cases undermine economic prosperity, but cleaning up office-selling could also harm the local economy, indicating a negative impact of personnel corruption that lingers over time. The negative effect of cleaning up office-selling is most likely to result from the "personnel earthquake" and political uncertainty following corruption crackdowns, which tend to disrupt business–government networks and

[35] Other types do not have sufficient data for panel data regressions.

discourage investment (Zhu & Zhang 2017a). In Models 5 and 6, the number of office-selling syndicates has a statistically significant negative association with local economic prosperity at both administrative levels. One additional office-selling case can reduce log local nighttime light brightness by 5.4–6.7% (i.e., more than 1% of light brightness), supporting my observation from case studies. While the regressions only show correlations, they suggest a strong tendency of office sales eroding economic development, and these impacts are very likely underestimated. Wu et al. (2022) have found that overall courts in wealthier eastern provinces tend to be more transparent. If this pattern holds, Dataset B can systematically undercount cases in less-developed regions. Such measurement error would create an attenuation bias, pushing the observed correlation between office-selling and poor economic outcomes closer to zero; the true negative correlation could be larger than what models in Table 7 can detect.

Moreover, with the rise of capital to influence political selection, candidates without abundant capital could be knocked out of the competition. Although this does not inevitably rule out merit and capital holders are not necessarily incompetent, a shrinking and rigid selection pool of the "purchase class" can still affect merit recruitment, the composition of the selectorate, and policy outcomes (Gallagher & Hanson 2013; Huang & Yang 2022). For instance, decision-makers arising from the purchase class could have narrower policy preferences favoring capital. Through what Shirk (2008) calls "reciprocal accountability" in a two-way power flow, the office buyers may also exercise some degree of influence on leaders "appointing" them and affect policymaking at higher levels. Even more importantly, money may increasingly replace common experiences and similar policy pursuits as the glue binding elites together. Elite alliances based on money may affect the fundamental logic of elite interactions, their cohesion, and regimes' capacity to deal with internal and external threats. Building on a dataset of 12,000 appointments in the People's Liberation Army, Mattingly (2024) rigorously shows that the Party leaders in China intentionally promote loyal officers to respond to domestic threats and competent officers in periods of foreign threat. However, if promotion *within* the military heavily relied on purchase, rather than competence or loyalty, only promoting loyal or competent officers may not effectively solve the foreign-domestic threat trade-off for the top leader.

6.2 Efforts to Combat Personnel Corruption by the CCP

The Chinese central authorities have demonstrated increasing awareness of personnel corruption in the past decades. The administration under President Xi Jinping has shown a particularly strong commitment to combating this kind of corruption. For instance, a search for the keywords "appointing and using personnel" (*xuanren*

Table 7 Personnel corruption's relationship with local economy at prefecture and county levels

	Dependent variables: Log light brightness					
	Model 1 prefecture	**Model 2 prefecture**	**Model 3 county**	**Model 4 county**	**Model 5 prefecture**	**Model 6 county**
Number of ongoing office-selling cases	−0.016** (0.003)		−0.003 (0.002)			
Number of arrested cases		−0.053** (0.027)		−0.041** (0.017)		
Number of office-selling syndicates					−0.067*** (0.021)	−0.054*** (0.015)
Control	Yes	Yes	Yes	Yes	Yes	Yes
Year fixed effect	Yes	Yes	Yes	Yes	Yes	Yes
Prefecture fixed effect	Yes	Yes	Yes	Yes	Yes	Yes
Constant	10.585** (4.502)	10.619** (4.512)	9.561*** (1.363)	9.586*** (1.366)	10.620** (4.511)	9.595*** (1.366)
Observations	2,536	2,536	11,390	11,390	2,536	11,390
R-squared	0.697	0.696	0.517	0.517	0.696	0.518
Number of local id	333	333	2,206	2,206	333	2,206

Notes: Robust standard errors in parentheses. *** $p < 0.01$, ** $p < 0.05$, * $p < 0.1$.

Source: Personnel corruption data are from Dataset B, and other data are from Landry, Lü, and Duan (2018).

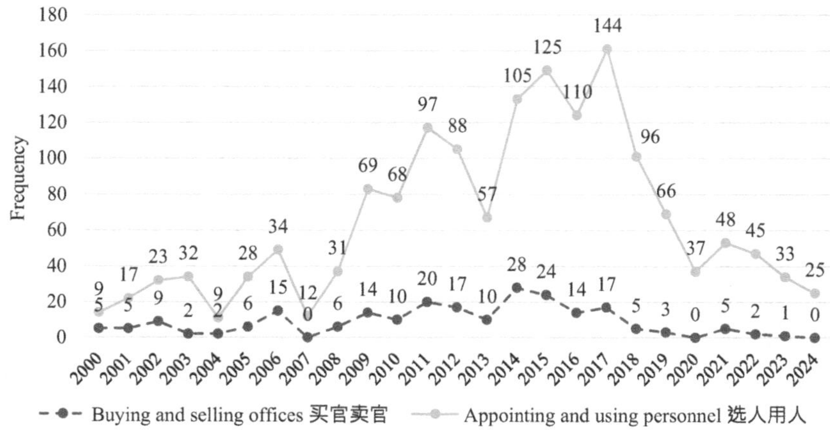

Figure 23 Keyword appearance frequencies in the *People's Daily*, 2000–24.

Source: Author's database.

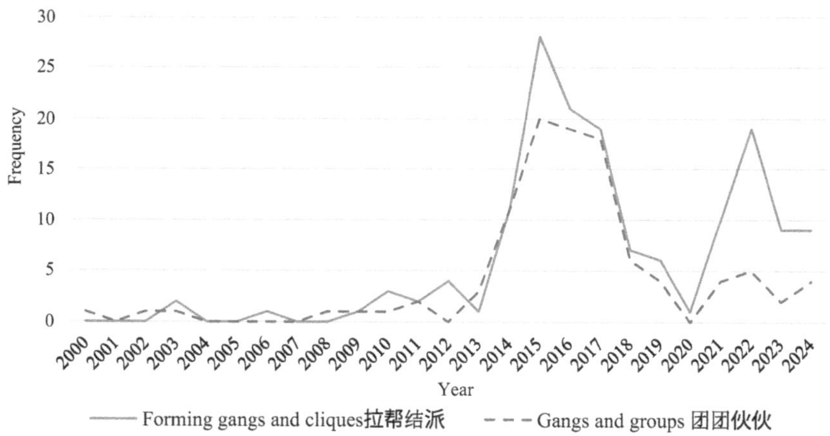

Figure 24 Frequency of keywords denouncing the formation of gangs and cliques in the *People's Daily*.

Source: Author's database.

yongren) and "buying and selling offices" (*maiguan maiguan*), the two phrases most frequently used in official talks on personnel corruption, in the *People's Daily* database shows a steadily increasing trend over time, with peaks between 2013 and 2017 – a period overlapping with the investigations of the mega tigers (Figure 23). Xi's administration has cracked down on oligarchical power bases in particular. For example, officials implicated in the wealth and power defense gangs of Zhou and Ling (Section 3) have all been arrested (Zhu, Huang, & Zhang 2019; Zhu 2022). As reflected in Figure 24, keywords such as "the formation of gangs and cliques" and "gangs and groups" have frequently appeared in the *People's Daily* articles, denouncing such activities since 2013, although several gangs formed considerably before Xi came into power.

The central inspection teams revived in the Xi era have been sent down from the Party center to provinces and centrally managed SOEs and public organizations since 2013 (Fu 2015; Yeo 2015). As emphasized by Wang Qishan, former secretary of the CCDI, the central inspection was intended to uncover problems, build up deterrence, and prevent corruption from spreading. One of the main forms of bureaucratic noncompliance on which the central inspection teams focused was corruption in personnel selection and appointment.[36]

In addition to corruption crackdowns, many state laws, Party laws (e.g., Party disciplines/ordinances), and government regulations have been stipulated by the Party center and the COD in the past decades to institutionalize cadre management and prevent personnel corruption. Figure 25 summarizes the major laws and guidelines on personnel management adopted by year. Online Appendix C lists the Chinese titles of the laws, their types (i.e., Party constitution, Party law, state law, regulation), their issuing authorities (e.g., Party center, COD), and aspects of cadre management under regulation (e.g., selection, appointment, election).

Figure 25 shows that, first, the central authorities of the CCP under the leadership of Xi emphasize cadre management. Eleven of the twenty laws are new laws stipulated after Xi assumed office. The other nine laws, adopted formally or in trial versions earlier, have also been revised, formalized, and detailed in recent years. The extensive legislation demonstrates the Chinese authorities' growing attention to the issue of personnel corruption and resolve to curb it. Many laws were directly issued by the Central Committee of the CCP or Party Center, indicating a top-down approach to personnel management and the high supervisory status of these regulations.

Second, these laws are comprehensively designed to complement each other in personnel management. The twenty laws cover all fourteen major aspects of cadre management, from recruitment to retirement. Cadre selection and appointment are the most regulated areas, with eleven laws specifically about them or having relevant rules. Another area also governed by eleven laws is supervision and disciplinary actions, indicating the Party's commitment to combating personnel corruption.

Third, law-making has shown a trend of gradual detailing and systematization. Including the twenty laws in Figure 25, more than 100 laws, regulations, rules, codes, and measures have been issued by different authorities at different levels. They regulate general and specific facets of personnel matters and implementation. Many particular problems targeted by the regulations, such

[36] See reports at www.ccdi.gov.cn/special/zyxszt/xwdt_zyxs/201402/t20140225_19064.html.

Figure 25 Major laws related to cadre management from 1980 to 2021, by the first adoption year.

as holiday gifts, election procedures, and nominations of candidates, indicate that higher-level governments are generally well informed about the common manifestations of personnel corruption in practice.

Finally, in terms of strategies to combat personnel corruption, these laws feature prohibitions of acts that create opportunities for buying and selling offices, standardization of decision-making processes, and guidance for cadres to properly pursue career advancement. For example, the Code of Conduct for the Discussion and Decision of Cadre Appointments and Removals by Party Committees (Party Groups) details specific situations in which discussions of a cadre's appointment and promotion are not allowed. The Regulations on the Election of Party Groups list in detail procedures for the standardization of personnel management to reduce institutional loopholes. In addition, innovations have been made to guide cadres away from the "rat race" that could lead to personnel corruption. For instance, the Regulations on the Parallel System of Civil Service Positions and Ranks transform a narrow path toward career advancement into a dual channel to promotion, aiming to untie cadres' career prospects, administrative ranks, salaries, and other benefits from scarce leadership positions. With the dual channel, competent cadres performing well in their jobs but not necessarily suitable to be leaders could still be awarded with incremental increases in rank and salary. This reform has been experimented with in selected government agencies since 2013 and is especially welcomed by young public servants (He 2016). Despite reasonable concerns, this reform may weaken some incentives for buying offices, such as the promotion ceilings discussed in Section 4.[37] Overall, while anticorruption is a major strategy used by the CCP to appease the public and boost political trust in China (e.g., O'Brien & Li 2006; Li 2025), the attention paid to buying and selling offices, particularly the oligarchical power bases, during corruption crackdowns shows that the Party-state considers this kind of corruption a major threat to the central authority and regime resilience.

6.3 Effects of Combating Buying and Selling Offices

Explicit sale of offices has occurred much less frequently since 2017 under Xi's large-scale anticorruption initiatives. According to government insiders I interviewed, few still dare to sell or buy public posts under the stringent anti-corruption efforts.[38] Their observations coincide with the reduced size of payments in revealed office-selling cases in Dataset B. As shown in Figure 26, the average size of payments increased from 2002 to 2010 and subsequently decreased significantly after 2013.

Figure 27 illustrates that the average price for political power after 2013 was less than half of that before 2013. Although the 2013 watershed may be due to the use of a smaller sample of personnel corruption cases post-2013, it is also possible that the intensive crackdown on corruption has deterred many officials from engaging in buying and selling offices, and only those with close personal ties are still opportunistic. However, the reduced supply and demand have decreased prices; furthermore, those engaged in the sale of offices might strategically exchange smaller amounts of money to evade penalties, especially

[37] Details of the regulations are at www.gov.cn/zhengce/2019-03/27/content_5377422.htm. Scholars raise concerns, including the long time to earn an increase in rank and salary and the significantly lower benefits of the policy for public servants aged forty years or older (He 2016).

[38] Interview conducted in July 2024.

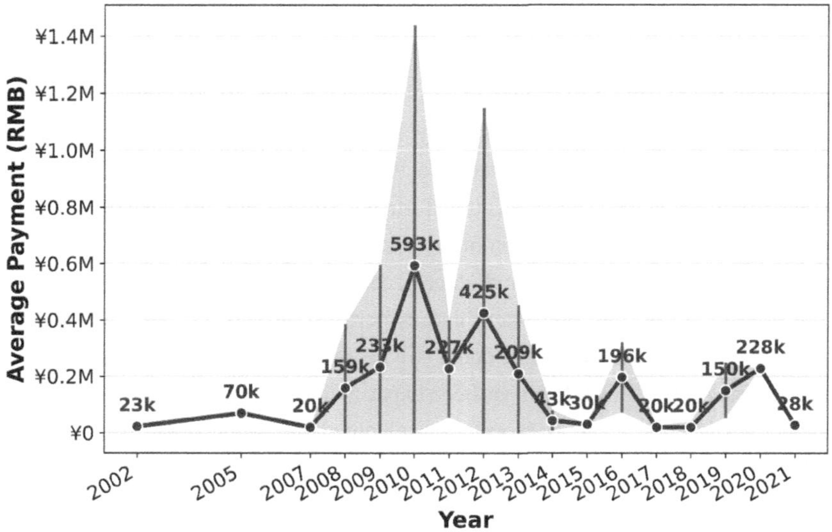

Figure 26 Average payment per purchase in RMB, 2002–21.

Note: The statistics here only consider cases that occurred in a single year. The blue shaded area shows the 95% confidence interval, not applicable to years with only one observation.

Source: Dataset B.

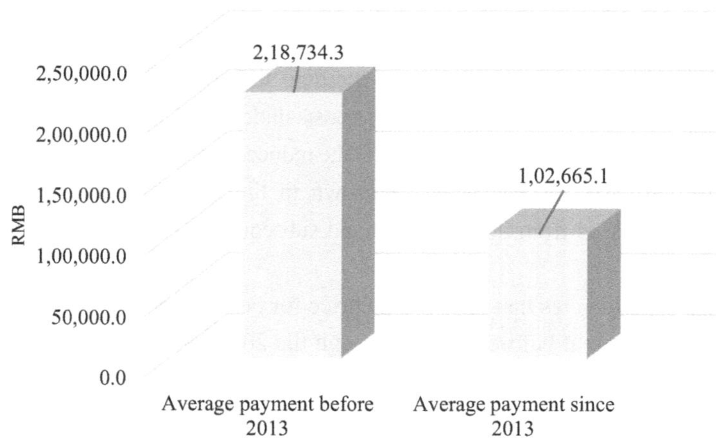

Figure 27 Average payment in RMB before and after 2013.

Source: Figure 26.

severe ones if caught, as the size of bribes seems to be a major factor affecting sentencing (Zhu 2012b; Gong, Wang & Li 2019). In Dataset B, several suspects in the court judgments reported returning bribes to office buyers, scared by the central inspection teams. These examples signal the effectiveness of the anti-corruption policies initiated by President Xi. As a former CDI head shared in an interview: "New corruption has been largely reduced and deterred under the current environment, while corruption accumulated from previous eras is still massive."[39]

6.4 Final Remarks

In a regime long understood to select officials based on performance or patronage, what is the role of money? This Element confronts this "elephant in the room" through a systematic examination of the buying and selling of government offices, or personnel corruption in China. Office-selling is not an isolated anomaly but a widespread phenomenon across different administrative levels, public sectors, and geographic localities, even evolving into highly organized forms. This finding reveals a significant blind spot under any analytical framework focused solely on the performance–patronage trade-off.

The core theoretical contribution of this Element is to propose *purchase* as a third, crucial paradigm to reimagine political selection in China. I construct a tripartite framework of performance, patronage, and purchase. This novel framework compels us to view officials at all levels as agents with their own political and economic interests, not merely as proxies of a higher authority. Consequently, the objective of political selection becomes more complex: It is not only about finding competence for the state or securing loyalty for a patron but also about a leader's opportunity to personally engage in rent-seeking and maximize financial gain. In fact, this study reveals that leaders often weigh three competing goals in personnel decisions: a subordinate's performance, their personal loyalty, and the leader's own monetary gain.

Under specific conditions, rent-maximizing can override the other two goals. For instance, a leader's incentive for rent-seeking through selling offices intensifies when their own promotion opportunities narrow. Alternatively, money can become the decisive factor that breaks a tie when candidates are otherwise difficult to distinguish in terms of their performance and loyalty under traditional evaluation systems. Thus, some of the elite promotion explained by the performance (competence)–patronage (loyalty) dichotomy in previous research may be confounded by office purchase, which is financially enabled and oriented.[40]

This dynamic interplay of the three logics explains why the sale of offices manifests in diverse forms. The four types of office-selling categorized in this

[39] Interview conducted in July 2024.

[40] Tentative regressions show that purchase explains some promotion outcomes.

study, from simple "primitive bribery" to complex "oligarchical powerbases," are effectively concrete projections of the tripartite framework in different contexts. For example, "office-selling syndicates" maximize the role of the purchase paradigm, creating a market-like exchange for political power. In contrast, "oligarchical powerbases" witness a deep fusion of purchase and patronage to serve the dual political goals of defending wealth and power.

A deeper insight is that money is not just capital to purchase a post; it also forges a new type of "loyalty," if it can be called so, distinct from traditional patronage. While traditional clientelism is often built on trust derived from shared experiences, the ties established through buying and selling offices may be sustained by transactional commitment or, in the case of oligarchies, evolve into a "coerced loyalty" based on mutual incrimination and blackmail. This distinction is critical for understanding the cohesion, behavior, and stability of different elite groups in Chinese politics.

The tripartite framework also offers a broad comparative lens, enabling a more nuanced cross-national and cross-regime analysis that moves beyond merely identifying the existence of buying and selling offices. The phenomenon has historical precedents in premodern Europe and imperial China; it is also pervasive in many postcommunist states, such as Russia, Azerbaijan, Ukraine, Georgia, and Kyrgyzstan, and developing countries such as Indonesia and India (Kristiansen & Ramli 2006; Engvall 2015). However, my framework still reveals that the relative weights of the purchase, patronage, and performance dimensions vary dramatically across contexts. For instance, in Kyrgyzstan, office purchase is highly transactional and market-driven, with less emphasis on loyalty; money functions as the primary currency. In contrast, in China and Indonesia, personal connections and loyalty remain critical gatekeepers, and the act of purchase is often deeply intertwined with the logic of patronage. This variation may reflect differing modes of authoritarian control and tolerance for corruption: a more openly permissive environment fosters purer market-based transactions, whereas periodic crackdowns compel corrupt activities to embed themselves within more clandestine relational networks (Engvall 2015; Berenschot 2018).

Going further, the framework can even bridge the study of democratic and authoritarian polities. The logic of the purchase paradigm is clearly visible in political selection in democracies, albeit in different forms. The case of former Illinois governor Rod Blagojevich, who attempted to sell Barack Obama's vacated Senate seat, reveals that selling office can emerge under any system. More universally, campaign fundraising in democracies, though legal, reflects the influence of the purchase paradigm in its essence. Scholars of American politics have long argued for the necessity of money for candidates to conduct political marketing (Thomsen 2023; Zeng 2024). A candidate's ability to raise funds often determines the scale and success of their campaign, thereby significantly shaping the electoral outcome before voters cast their ballots (Thomsen 2023). Thus, both illicit office-selling in authoritarian regimes and legal campaign fundraising in democracies underscore a common characteristic of elite politics that transcends regime type: Resource disparities influence power distribution even before power is formally distributed.

Ultimately, this systematic study of buying and selling offices exposes the inherent tensions within the Chinese state, where a meritocratic state prioritizing competence, a clientelist state emphasizing loyalty, and an investment state bound by money coexist and compete. Moreover, the investment state operates in a predatory and expansionary manner, driven by office buyers' urge to recoup their "investment." The experiences of other countries show that attempts to combat personnel corruption by simply codifying merit-based selection and promotion are unlikely to succeed when all positions are considered for sale (Engvall 2015). The Xi administration's aggressive anticorruption endeavors, particularly its crackdown on "oligarchical powerbases," can be seen as an effort by the central authority to curb the unrestrained expansion of the "predatory investment state" and reassert the dominance of the meritocratic and Party-defined clientelist states. However, historical precedents caution that closing off a widely used pathway for elite upward mobility may alienate mediocre officials who stand out in neither competence nor loyalty (Zhang 2022). The true challenge for the Chinese government, therefore, lies not only in eradicating the path of purchase but also in dynamically managing all three pathways to power to maintain the vitality of its elite corps and the resilience of the regime.

References

Adkins, Randall E., and Andrew J. Dowdle. 2002. "The Money Primary: What Influences the Outcome of Pre-Primary Presidential Nomination Fundraising?" *Presidential Studies Quarterly*, vol. 32, no.2: 256–275.

Albanese, Jay S. 2000. "The Causes of Organized Crime: Do Criminals Organize around Opportunities for Crime or Do Criminal Opportunities Create New Offenders?" *Journal of Contemporary Criminal Justice*, vol. 16, no. 4: 409–423.

Allen, Douglas W. 2005. "Purchase, Patronage, and Professions: Incentives and the Evolution of Public Office in Pre-Modern Britain," *Journal of Institutional and Theoretical Economics*, March, vol. 161, no. 1: 57–79.

Ang, Yuen Yuen. 2020. *China's Gilded Age: The Paradox of Economic Boom and Vast Corruption*. Cambridge: Cambridge University Press.

Benzel, Ed. 2024. "Loyalty." *World Neurosurgery*, vol. 183: xix.

Berenschot, Ward. 2018. "Incumbent Bureaucrats: Why Elections Undermine Civil Service Reform in Indonesia." *Public Administration and Development*, vol. 38, no. 4: 135–143.

Besley, Timothy. 2005. "Political Selection." *Journal of Economic Perspectives*, vol. 19, no. 3: 43–60.

Best, Shaun. 2002. *Introduction to Politics and Society*. London, UK: Sage Publications.

Bird, Rebecca B., and Eric Alden Smith. 2005. "Signaling Theory, Strategic Interaction, and Symbolic Capital." *Current Anthropology*, vol. 46, no. 2: 221–248.

Boucek, Francois. 2009. "Rethinking Factionalism: Typologies, Intra-Party Dynamics and Three Faces of Factionalism." *Party Politics*, vol. 15, no. 4: 455–485.

Brunetti, Aymo, and Beatrice Weder. 2003. "A Free Press Is Bad News for -Corruption." *Journal of Public Economics*, vol. 87, nos. 7–8: 1801–1824.

Burns, John, and Xiaoqi Wang. 2010. "Civil Service Reform in China: Impacts on Civil Servants' Behaviour." *The China Quarterly*, vol. 201: 58–78.

Cai, Yongshun. 2014. *State and Agents in China: Disciplining Government Officials*. Stanford, CA: Stanford University Press.

Chan, Hon S., and Jie Gao. 2008. "Performance Measurement in Chinese Local Governments." *Chinese Law and Government*, vol. 41, nos. 2–3: 4–9.

Chen, Shuo, and Yiran Li. 2024. "Accountability from Cyberspace? Scandal Exposure on the Internet and Official Governance in China." *Political Science Research and Methods*, vol. 12, no. 1: 130–145.

Chen, Ting, and James Kai-Sing Kung. 2019. "Busting the 'Princelings': The Campaign against Corruption in China's Primary Land Market." *The Quarterly Journal of Economics*, vol. 9: 185–226.

Chen, Ting, and Ji Yeon Hong. 2021. "Rivals within: Political Factions, Loyalty, and Elite Competition under Authoritarianism." *Political Science Research and Methods*, vol. 9, no. 3: 599–614.

Choi, Eun Kyong. 2012. "Patronage and Performance: Factors in the Political Mobility of Provincial Leaders in Post-Deng China." *The China Quarterly*, vol. 212: 965–981.

Darden, Keith A. 2001. "Blackmail as a Tool of State Domination: Ukraine under Kuchma." *East European Constitutional Review*, vol. 10, nos. 2–3: 67–71.

Dickson, Bruce J. 2003. *Red Capitalists in China*. Cambridge, England: Cambridge University Press.

Doyle, William. 1996. *Venality: The Sale of Offices in Eighteenth-Century France*. Oxford: Clarendon Press.

Doyon, Jérôme. 2018. "Clientelism by Design: Personnel Politics under Xi Jinping." *Journal of Current Chinese Affairs*, vol. 47, no. 3: 87–110.

Doyon, Jérôme, and Franziska Barbara Keller. 2020. "Knowing the Wrong Cadre? Networks and Promotions in the Chinese Party-State." *Political Studies*, vol. 68, no. 4: 1036–1053.

Edin, Maria. 1998. "Why Do Chinese Local Cadres Promote Growth? Institutional Incentives and Constraints of Local Cadres." *Forum for Development Studies*, vol. 25, no. 1: 97–127.

Edin, Maria. 2003. "State Capacity and Local Agent Control in China: CCP Cadre Management from a Township Perspective." *The China Quarterly*, vol. 173: 35–52.

Egorov, Georgy, and Konstantin Sonin. 2011. "Dictators and Their Viziers: Endogenizing the Loyalty–Competence Tradeoff." *Journal of the European Economic Association*, vol. 9, no. 5: 903–930.

Engvall, Johan. 2015. "The State as Investment Market: A Framework for Interpreting the Post-Soviet State in Eurasia." *Governance*, vol. 28, no. 1: 25–40.

Feng, Bo, Xi Weng, and Qi Zhang. 2024. "Building a Loyal and Cohesive Team of Your Own: A Screening-Based Theory of Faction Formation." *Working paper.*

Feng, Junqi. 2010. 中县干部 *(Cadres of County Zhong)*. Doctoral Dissertation, Peking University.

Fletcher, George P. 1993. *Loyalty: An Essay on the Morality of Relationships*. New York: Oxford University Press.

Fouirnaies, Alexander. 2021. "How Do Campaign Spending Limits Affect Elections? Evidence from the United Kingdom 1885–2019." *American Political Science Review*, vol. 115, no. 2: 395–411.

Freedman, Paul, Michael Franz, and Kenneth Goldstein. 2004. "Campaign Advertising and Democratic Citizenship." *American Journal of Political Science*, vol. 48, no. 4: 723–741.

Fu, Hualing. 2015. Wielding the Sword: President Xi's New Anti-corruption Campaign. In *Greed, Corruption, and the Modern State: Essays in Political Economy*, edited by Susan Rose-Ackerman and Paul Lagunes, 134–158. Cheltenham: Edward Elgar.

Gallagher, Mary, and Jonathan K. Hanson. 2013. Authoritarian Survival, Resilience, and the Selectorate Theory. In *Why Communism Did Not Collapse: Understanding Authoritarian Regime Resilience in Asia and Europe*, edited by Martin K. Dimitrov, 185–204. New York: Cambridge University Press.

Gong, Ting. 1994. *The Politics of Corruption in Contemporary China: An Analysis of Policy Outcomes*. Westport: Praeger.

Gong, Ting. 2002. "Dangerous Collusion: Corruption as a Collective Venture in Contemporary China." *Communist and Post-Communist Studies*, vol. 35, no. 1: 85–103.

Gong, Ting, Shiru Wang, and Hui Li. 2019. "Sentencing Disparities in Corruption Cases in China." *Journal of Contemporary China*, vol. 28, no. 116: 245–259.

Gong, Ting, and Muluan Wu. 2012. "我国2000 – 2009年腐败案例研究报告– –基于2800余个报道案例的分析 (Research Report on Corruption Cases in China from 2000 to 2009 – An Analysis Based on Over 2,800 Reported Cases)." 社会学研究 *(Sociology Studies)*, vol. 4: 204–220.

Guardado, Jenny. 2018. "Office-Selling, Corruption, and Long-Term Development in Peru," *American Political Science Review*, vol. 112, no. 4: 971–995.

Guo, Gang. 2009. "China's Local Political Budget Cycles." *American Journal of Political Science*, vol. 53, no. 3: 621–632.

Guo, Xuezhi. 2014. "Controlling Corruption in the Party: China's Central Discipline Inspection Commission." *The China Quarterly*, vol. 219: 597–624.

Guo, Yong. 2008. "Corruption in Transitional China: An Empirical Analysis." *The China Quarterly*, vol. 194: 349–364.

Hasker, Kevin, and Cagla Okten. 2008. "Intermediaries and Corruption." *Journal of Economic Behavior & Organization*, vol. 67, no. 1: 103–115.

He, Xian. 2016. "Study of Civil Servants Posts and Ranks Parallel System." *Chinese Public Administration*, vol. 9: 12–17.

Hodgson, Geoffrey M. 2014. "What is Capital? Economists and Sociologists Have Changed Its Meaning: Should It Be Changed Back?" *Cambridge Journal of Economics*, vol. 38: 1063–1086.

Huang, Yasheng, and Clair Yang. 2022. "A Longevity Mechanism of Chinese Absolutism." *Journal of Politics*, vol. 84, no. 2: 1165–1175.

Hurst, Charles E. 2007. *Social Inequality: Forms, Causes, and Consequences* (6th ed.). Boston, MA: Allyn and Bacon.

Jia, Linan. 2022. "Loyalty and Competence: The Political Selection of Local Cadres in China." *The China Quarterly*, vol. 251: 726–750.

Jia, Ruixue, Masayuki Kudamatsu, and David Seim. 2015. "Political Selection in China: The Complementary Roles of Connections and Performance." *Journal of the European Economic Association*, vol. 13, no. 4: 631–668.

Jiang, Junyan. 2018. "Making Bureaucracy Work: Patronage Networks, Performance Incentives, and Economic Development in China." *American Journal of Political Science*, vol. 62, no. 4: 982–999.

Jiang, Junyan, and Songbo Yang. 2024. "Physiognomic Features and the Tacit Domain of Political Selection in China." Paper presented at the Annual Meeting of the American Political Science Association, Philadelphia, PA.

Kang, Siqin, and Jiangnan Zhu. 2021. "Do People Trust the Government More? Unpacking the Distinct Impacts of Anticorruption Policies on Political Trust." *Political Research Quarterly*, vol. 74, no. 2: 434–449.

Kaufmann, Daniel, Sanjay Pradhan, and Randi Ryterman. 1998. *New Frontiers in Diagnosing and Combating Corruption*. World Bank. https://documents1.worldbank.org/curated/en/185671468029363673/pdf/18572-BRI-REPLACEMENT-premnote7-PUBLIC.pdf.

Keller, Franziska B. 2016. "Moving beyond Factions: Using Social Network Analysis to Uncover Patronage Networks among Chinese Elites." *Journal of East Asian Studies*, vol. 16, no. 1: 17–41.

Key, V. O. 1956. *American State Politics: An Introduction*. New York: Alfred A. Knopf.

Ko, Kilkon, and Cuifen Weng. 2011. "Critical Review of Conceptual Definitions of Chinese Corruption: a formal–legal perspective." *Journal of Contemporary China*, vol. 20, no.70: 359–378.

Ko, Kilkon, and Cuifen Weng. 2012. "Structural Changes in Chinese Corruption." *The China Quarterly*, vol. 211: 718–740.

Kostka, Genia, and Xiaofan Yu. 2015. "Career Backgrounds of Municipal Party Secretaries in China: Why Do So Few Municipal Party Secretaries Rise from the County Level?" *Modern China*, vol. 41, no. 5: 467–505.

Kou, Chien-Wen, and Wen-Hsuan Tsai. 2014. "'Sprinting with Small Steps' Towards Promotion: Solutions for the Age Dilemma in the CCP Cadre Appointment System." *The China Journal*, vol. 71, no. 1: 153–171.

Kraus, Willy. 1991. *Private Business in China: Revival between Ideology and Pragmatism*. Honolulu: University of Hawaii Press.

Kristiansen, Stein, and Muhid Ramli. 2006. "Buying an Income: The Market for Civil Service Positions in Indonesia." *Contemporary Southeast Asia*, vol. 28, no. 2: 207–233.

Lammers, Joris, Adam D. Galinsky, Derek D. Rucker, and Jennifer A. Magee. 2016. "To Have Control Over or to Be Free from Others? The Desire for Power Reflects a Need for Autonomy." *Personality and Social Psychology Bulletin*, vol. 42, no. 4: 498–512.

Landry, Pierre F., Xiaobo Lü, and Haiyan Duan. 2018. "Does Performance Matter? Evaluating Political Selection along the Chinese Administrative Ladder." *Comparative Political Studies*, vol. 51, no. 8: 1074–1105.

Leff, Nathaniel H. 1964. "Economic Development through Bureaucratic Corruption." *American Behavioral Scientist*, vol. 8, no. 3: 8–14.

Li, Cheng. 2001. *China's Leaders: The New Generation*. Lanham: Rowman & Littlefield.

Li, Cheng. 2012. "The End of the CCP's Resilient Authoritarianism? A Tripartite Assessment of Shifting Power in China." *The China Quarterly*, vol. 211: 595–623.

Li, Hui, and Wenyan Tu. 2024. "Induction, Immersion, and the Life-Cycle of Corruption: How Social Interactions Affect Temporal Factors in Corruption Behavior." *Chinese Journal of Sociology*, vol. 44, no. 5: 125–159.

Li, Lianjiang. 2025. *Political Trust in China*. Ann Arbor, MI: University of Michigan Press.

Li, Zeren, and Melanie Manion. 2023. "The Decline of Factions: The Impact of a Broad Purge on Political Decision Making in China." *British Journal of Political Science*, vol. 53, no. 3: 815–834.

Liebert, Saltanat. 2014. "Challenges of Reforming the Civil Service in the Post-Soviet Era: The Case of Kyrgyzstan." *Review of Public Personnel Administration*, vol. 34, no. 4: 403–420.

Lieberthal, Kenneth, and Michel Oksenberg. 1988. *Policy Making in China: Leaders, Structures, and Processes*. Princeton, NJ: Princeton University Press.

Liebman, Benjamin L., Margaret E. Roberts, Rachel E. Stern, and Alice Z. Wang. 2020. "Mass Digitization of Chinese Court Decisions: How to Use Text as Data in the Field of Chinese Law." *Journal of Law and Courts*, vol. 8, no. 2: 177–201.

Lin, Qinnan. 2021. "刑事裁判文书上网公开制度的实践及反思 (Practice and Reflection on the Online Disclosure System of Criminal Judgments)." 福建农林大学学报*(哲学社会科学版) (Journal of Fujian Agriculture and Forestry University, Philosophy and Social Sciences Edition)*, vol. 24, no. 5: 89–97.

Lin, Wanlin, Siqin Kang, Jiangnan Zhu, and Li Ding. 2025. “Till We Have Red Faces: Drinking to Signal Trustworthiness in Contemporary China.” *Public Choice*, vol. 203, 3–22.

Lü, Xiaobo. 2000. *Cadres and Corruption: The Organizational Involution of the Chinese Communist Party.* Stanford, CA: Stanford University Press.

Ma, Chao, Xiaohong Yu, and Haibo He. 2016. “大数据分析:中国司法裁判文书上网公开报告 (Big Data Analysis: Report on the Online Disclosure of Chinese Judicial Verdict Documents).” 中国法律评论 *(Chinese Law Review)*, vol. 4: 195–246.

Manion, Melanie. 1985. “The Cadre Management System, Post-Mao: The Appointment, Promotion, Transfer and Removal of Party and State Leaders.” *The China Quarterly*, vol. 102: 203–233.

Manion, Melanie. 2004. *Corruption by Design: Building Clean Government in Mainland China and Hong Kong*. Cambridge, MA: Harvard University Press.

Manion, Melanie. 2023. *Political Selection in China: Rethinking Foundations and Findings*. Cambridge: Cambridge University Press.

Mattingly, Daniel C. 2024. “How the Party Commands the Gun: The Foreign–Domestic Threat Dilemma in China.” *American Journal of Political Science*, vol. 68, no. 1: 227–242.

Mauro, Paolo, and David D. Driscoll. 1997. *Why Worry about Corruption?* Washington, DC: International Monetary Fund.

Méon, Pierre-Guillaume, and Khalid Sekkat. 2005. “Does Corruption Grease or Sand the Wheels of Growth?” *Public Choice*, vol. 122, no. 1: 69–97.

Meyer, David, Victor C. Shih, and Jonghyuk Lee. 2016. “Factions of Different Stripes: Gauging the Recruitment Logics of Factions in the Reform Period.” *Journal of East Asian Studies*, vol. 16, no. 1: 43–60.

Miller, Michael K. 2015. “Elections, Information, and Policy Responsiveness in Autocratic Regimes.” *Comparative Political Studies*, vol. 48, no. 6: 691–727.

Nathan, Andrew J. 1973. “A Factionalism Model for CCP Politics.” *The China Quarterly*. vol. 53: 34–66.

Nathan, Andrew J., and Kellee S. Tsai. 1995. “Factionalism: A New Institutionalist Restatement.” *The China Journal*, vol. 34: 157–192.

O’Brien, Kevin J., and Lianjiang Li. 2006. *Rightful Resistance in Rural China*. New York: Cambridge University Press.

Oi, Jean. 1999. *Rural China Takes Off: Institutional Foundations of Economic Reform*. Berkeley, CA: University of California Press.

Pang, Baoqing, Shu Keng, and Lingna Zhong. 2018. “Sprinting with Small Steps: China’s Cadre Management and Authoritarian Resilience.” *The China Journal*, vol. 80, no. 1: 68–93.

Pearson, Margaret. 1997. *China's New Business Elite*. Berkeley: University of California Press.

Pearson, Margaret M., Meg Rithmire, and Kellee Tsai. 2023. *The State and Capitalism in China*. New York: Cambridge University Press.

Pei, Minxin. 2016. *China's Crony Capitalism: The Dynamics of Regime Decay*. Cambridge, MA: Harvard University Press.

Pérez-Durán, Ixcehl. 2023. "Twenty-Five Years of Accountability Research in Public Administration: Authorship, Themes, Methods, and Future Trends." *International Review of Administrative Sciences*, vol. 90, no. 3: 546–562.

Pieke, Frank N. 2009. *The Good Communist: Elite Training and State Building in Today's China*. New York: Cambridge University Press.

Pye, Lucian W. 1981. *The Dynamics of Chinese Politics*. Cambridge, Mass.: Oelgeschlager, Gunn & Hain.

Qian, Jingyuan, and Steve Bai. 2024. "The Zeal of the Outgroup: Loyalty Signaling, Bureaucratic Compliance, and Variation of State Repression in Authoritarian Regimes." *Comparative Politics*, vol. 56, no. 4: 423–447.

Reno, William. 1995. *Corruption and State Politics in Sierra Leone*. Cambridge: Cambridge University Press.

Rithmire, Meg, and Hao Chen. 2021. "The Emergence of Mafia-Like Business Systems in China." *The China Quarterly*, vol. 248, no. 1: 1037–1058.

Rose-Ackerman, Susan. 1999. *Corruption and Government: Causes, Consequences, and Reform*. New York: Cambridge University Press.

Roth, Mitchel P., and Murat Sever. 2007. "The Kurdish Workers Party (PKK) as Criminal Syndicate: Funding Terrorism through Organized Crime, a Case Study." *Studies in Conflict & Terrorism*, vol. 30, no. 10: 901–920.

Schelling, Thomas C. 1971. "What Is the Business of Organized Crime?" *The American Scholar*, vol. 40, no. 4: 643–652.

Scott, Ian, and Ting Gong. 2015. "Evidence-Based Policy-Making for Corruption Prevention in Hong Kong: A Bottom-Up Approach." *Asia Pacific Journal of Public Administration*, vol. 37, no. 2: 87–101.

Scott, James C. 1969. "Corruption, Machine Politics, and Political Change." *American Political Science Review*, vol. 63, no. 4: 1142–1158.

Shih, Victor. 2004. "Factions Matter: Personal Networks and the Distribution of Bank Loans in China." *Journal of Contemporary China*, vol. 13, no. 38: 3–19.

Shih, Victor. 2008. *Factions and Finance in China: Elite Conflict and Inflation*. Cambridge: Cambridge University Press.

Shih, Victor, and Jonghyuk Lee. 2020. "Locking in Fair Weather Friends: Assessing the Fate of Chinese Communist Elite When Their Patrons Fall from Power." *Party Politics*, vol. 26, no. 5: 628–639.

Shih, Victor, Christopher Adolph, and Mingxing Liu. 2012. "Getting Ahead in the Communist Party: Explaining the Advancement of Central Committee Members in China." *American Political Science Review*, vol. 106, no. 1: 166–187.

Shirk, Susan L. 2008. *China: Fragile Superpower*. New York: Oxford University Press.

Smith, Lionel. 2020. "Loyalty." *McGill Law Journal*, vol. 66, no. 1: 121–125.

Solinger, Dorothy J. 1992. "Urban Bureaucrats and the State: The Merger of State and Society." In *State and Society in China: The Consequences of Reform*, edited by Arthur Lewis Rosenbaum, pp. 127–146. Boulder: Westview Press.

Souryal, Sam S., and Brian W. McKay. 1996. "Personal Loyalty to Superiors in Public Service." *Criminal Justice Ethics*, vol. 15, no. 2: 44–62.

Stern, Rachel E., Benjamin L. Liebman, Margaret E. Roberts, and Alice Z. Wang. 2021. "Automating Fairness? Artificial Intelligence in the Chinese Courts." *Columbia Journal of Transnational Law*, vol. 59: 515.

Sun, Xin. 2015. "Selective Enforcement of Land Regulations: Why Large-Scale Violators Succeeded?" *The China Journal*, vol. 74, no. 2: 66–90.

Sun, Xin, Jiangnan Zhu, and Yiping Wu. 2014. "Organizational Clientelism: An Analysis of Private Entrepreneurs in Chinese Local Legislatures." *Journal of East Asian Studies*, vol. 14, no. 1: 1–29.

Sun, Yan. 2004. *Corruption and Market in Contemporary China*. Ithaca, NY: Cornell University Press.

Svolik, Milan W. 2012. *The Politics of Authoritarian Rule*. Cambridge University Press.

Thomsen, Danielle M. 2023. "Competition in Congressional Elections: Money versus Votes." *American Political Science Review*, vol. 117, no. 2: 675–691.

Tsai, Kellee S. 2006. "Adaptive Informal Institutions and Endogenous Institutional Change in China." *World Politics*, vol. 59, no. 1: 116–141.

Tsai, Wen-Hsuan, and Chien-Wen Kou. 2015. "The Party's Disciples: CCP Reserve Cadres and the Perpetuation of a Resilient Authoritarian Regime." *The China Quarterly*, vol. 221: 1–20.

Wade, Robert. 1985. "The Market for Public Office: Why the Indian State Is Not Better at Development." *World Development*, vol. 13, no. 4: 467–497.

Wallace, Jeremy. 2016. "Juking the Stats? Authoritarian Information Problems in China." *British Journal of Political Science*, vol. 46, no. 1: 11–29.

Wang, Peng. 2016. "Military Corruption in China: The Role of Guanxi in the Buying and Selling of Military Positions." *The China Quarterly*, vol. 228: 970–991.

Wang, Yuhua. 2013. "Court Funding and Judicial Corruption in China." *The China Journal*, vol. 69: 43–63.

Wang, Yuhua, and Carl Minzner. 2015. "The Rise of the Chinese Security State." *The China Quarterly*, vol. 222: 339–359.

Wang, Yuhua, and Bruce Dickson. 2022. "How Corruption Investigations Undermine Regime Support: Evidence from China." *Political Science Research and Methods*, vol. 10, no. 1: 33–48.

Wang, Zhenyu M., Tao Li, and Rodrigo Praino. 2024. "Is There a Prototype Leader Look? Evidence from the Photos of Chinese Local Leaders." *The Leadership Quarterly*, vol. 35, no. 4: 1–22.

Wank, David. 2001. *Commodifying Communism*. New York, NY: Cambridge University Press.

Weber, Max. 2013. *From Max Weber: Essays in Sociology*. London: Routledge.

Wedeman, Andrew. 2004. "The Intensification of Corruption in China." *The China Quarterly*, vol. 18: 895–921.

Wedeman, Andrew. 2012. *Double Paradox: Rapid Growth and Rising Corruption in China*. Ithaca, NY: Cornell University Press.

Wedeman, Andrew. 2017. "Xi Jinping's Tiger Hunt: Anti-Corruption Campaign or Political Purge?" *Modern China Studies*, vol. 24, no. 2: 35–82.

Wedeman, Andrew. 2022. "The Dynamics and Trajectory of Corruption in Contemporary China." *The China Review*, vol.22, no. 2: 21–48.

Whiting, Susan. 2001. *Power and Wealth in Rural China: The Political Economy of Institutional Change*. Cambridge: Cambridge University Press.

Whiting, Susan. 2004. "The Cadre Evaluation System at the Grass Roots: The Paradox of Party Rule." In *Holding China Together: Diversity and National Integration in the Post-Deng Era*, Barry Naughton and Dali Yang, pp. 101–119. Cambridge: Cambridge University Press.

Whitson, William, and Zhenxia Huang. 1973. *The Chinese High Command: A History of Communist Military Politics, 1927–71*. New York: Praeger.

Wiebe, Michael. 2020. Essays in Chinese Political Economy. *Doctoral Dissertation*, University of British Columbia.

Winters, Jeffrey A. 2011. *Oligarchy*. New York: Cambridge University Press.

Wintrobe, Ronald. 1998. *The Political Economy of Dictatorship*. Cambridge University Press.

Wong, Stan H., and Yu Zeng. 2017. "Do Inferences of Competence from Faces Predict Political Selection in Authoritarian Regimes? Evidence from China." *Social Science Research*, vol. 66 (August): 248–263.

Wu, Xiaohan, Margaret E. Roberts, Rachel E. Stern et al. 2022. "Augmenting Serialized Bureaucratic Data: The Case of Chinese Courts," *21st Century China Center Research Paper No. 2022-11*: 1–51.

Wu, Yu-Shan. 2015. "Rejuvenation of the Party-State: The Virtues and Limits of an Age-Based Political System." *Issues and Studies*, vol. 51, no. 1: 99.

Xiao, Hanyu, Ting Gong, and Wenyan Tu. 2024. "Why Trust Weighs More? Investigating the Endogenous Relationship between Trust and Perceived Institutional Effectiveness." *Administration & Society*. vol. 56, no. 5: 602–627. https://doi.org/10.1177/00953997241239000.

Yan, Yang, and Chunhui Yuan. 2020. "City Administrative Level and Municipal Party Secretaries' Promotion: Understanding the Logic of Shaping Political Elites in China." *Journal of Contemporary China*, vol. 29, no. 122: 266–285.

Yang, Dali, Huayu Xu, and Ran Tao. 2014. "A Tragedy of the Nomenklatura? Career Incentives, Political Loyalty and Political Radicalism during China's Great Leap Forward." *Journal of Contemporary China*, vol. 23, no. 89: 864–883.

Yeo, Yukyung. 2015. "Complementing the Local Discipline Inspection Commissions of the CCP: Empowerment of the Central Inspection Groups. *Journal of Contemporary China*, vol. 25, no. 97: 59–74.

Young, Susan. 1995. *Private Business and Economic Reform in China*. Armonk, NY: M. E. Sharpe.

Zeng, Yu. 2024. "Political Marketing in a Hierarchy: Media's Scorekeeping Role in China." *Working paper*.

Zeng, Yu, and Stan Hok-Wui Wong. 2021. "Time Is Power: Rethinking Meritocratic Political Selection in China." *The China Quarterly*, vol. 245: 23–50.

Zhang, Changdong. 2021. *Governing and Ruling: The Political Logic of Taxation in China*. Ann Arbor, MI: University of Michigan Press.

Zhang, Lawrence. 2022. *Power for a Price: The Purchase of Official Appointments in Qing China*. Cambridge, MA: Harvard University Press.

Zhong, Yang. 2015. *Local Government and Politics in China: Challenges from Below*. New York: Routledge.

Zhu, Jiangnan. 2008. "Why Are Offices for Sale in China? A Case Study of the Office-Selling Chain in Heilongjiang Province." *Asian Survey*, vol. 48, no. 4: 558–579.

Zhu, Jiangnan. 2012a. "The Shadow of the Skyscrapers: Real Estate Corruption in China." *Journal of Contemporary China*, vol. 21, no. 74: 243–260.

Zhu, Jiangnan. 2012b. "Do Severe Penalties Deter Corruption? A Game Theoretic Analysis of the Chinese Case." *The China Review*, vol. 12, no. 2: 1–32.

Zhu, Jiangnan. 2014. Corruption in Reform Era: A Multidisciplinary Review, in *The Sage Handbook of Contemporary China*, edited by Weiping Wu and Mark Frazier, 302–323. Los Angeles: Sage

Zhu, Jiangnan. 2022. "The Rise and Fall of Ruling Oligarchs." *The China Review*, vol. 22, no. 2: 49–79.

Zhu, Jiangnan, Huang Huang, and Dong Zhang. 2019. "'Big Tigers, Big Data': Learning Social Reactions to China's Anticorruption Campaign through Online Feedback." *Public Administration Review*, vol. 79, no. 4: 500–513.

Zhu, Jiangnan, and Yiping Wu. 2014. "Who Pays More 'Tributes' to the Government? Sectoral Corruption of China's Private Enterprises." *Crime, Law and Social Change*, vol. 64: 309–333.

Zhu, Jiangnan, and Dong Zhang. 2017a. "Does Corruption Hinder Private Businesses? Leadership Stability and Predictable Corruption in China." *Governance*, vol. 30, no. 3: 343–363.

Zhu, Jiangnan, and Dong Zhang. 2017b. "Weapons of the Powerful: Authoritarian Elite Competition and Politicized Anticorruption in China." *Comparative Political Studies*, vol. 50, no. 9: 1186–1220.

Zhu, Lin. 2015. "Punishing Corrupt Officials in China." *The China Quarterly*. vol. 223: 595–617.

Zuo, Cai (Vera). 2015. "Promoting City Leaders: The Structure of Political Incentives in China." *The China Quarterly*, vol. 224: 955–984.

Acknowledgments

The origins of this Element can be traced back more than twenty years, to my doctoral studies, when I first explored the complex interplay between corruption and officials' career advancement in China. Over the years, I have never let go of the idea of returning to those questions and developing them into a fuller work. This Element carries forward the central insight of my early work, enriched by the intervening years of research, reflection, and reimagination of (anti)corruption and elite politics in China. It embodies a long-cherished aspiration and affirms my belief: what we hold onto with sincerity and persistence will, in time, find its voice.

This Element could not have been completed without the support of many individuals. I am deeply indebted to Victor Shih for his exemplary guidance; to John Burns, Ruolin Su, and Qi Zhang for their generous suggestions, which have sharpened my thinking; and to colleagues at my university – Hualing Fu, Enze Han, Danny Lam, Cheng Li, George Lin, Lianjiang Li, Uwe Steinhoff, Robert Thomson, and Ming Wen – for their consistent encouragement. This work also benefited enormously from the invaluable feedback on earlier drafts presented at numerous institutions. I am particularly grateful to the following scholars and their students: Xin Sun at King's College London; Ting Gong at Southern University of Science and Technology; Chuanmin Chen, Haiyan Duan, Haibin Yan, and Duancheng Yang at East China University of Political Science and Law; Huirong Chen, Zhenhuan Lei, Yingjie Wei, Yu Zeng, Zhiyuan Zhang, and Siyao Zheng at Shanghai Jiaotong University; Yong Guo and Wei Song at Tsinghua University; and Juan Wang at McGill University. I also wish to thank Steve Bai, Jiaqi Chen, Jiawei Hai, Jianbing Li, Li Liao, Siqin Kang, Da'an Wang, Hanyu Xiao, Litianqing Yang, Wencong Yu, Minjun Yuan, Yu Zeng at Peking University, Dong Zhang, Hua Zhang, Yuxuan Zhang, and Yifei Zhu for their insightful comments, steadfast support, and timely assistance at various stages of this research. Many of my capstone students offered excellent research assistance, including Bosco Chan, Justin Chan, Jiarui Chang, Edmund Choi, Henry Chu, Pakenas Kajus, Kyra Krall, Ainsley Lai, Sylvia Lau, Micheal Lui, Ken Ng, Ashley Sit, Bella Tam, Kyle Tse, Amy Wan, Victor Yang, Prudence Yeung, Ariel Yip, and Jeria Yip.

I am also very grateful to the two anonymous reviewers for their close reading and constructive comments, and to Daniel Mattingly for his profound suggestions and prompt help, as well as the editors of the Cambridge University Press for their editorial assistance. I also acknowledge with gratitude the financial support of the General Research Fund (no. 17600225) awarded by the Research Grants Council of Hong Kong, which accorded this project its highest funding priority. Finally, I dedicate this Element to my family, whose patience, encouragement, and unwavering belief in the value of my work have sustained me throughout this journey.

Cambridge Elements

Chinese Economy and Governance

Luke Qi Zhang

Fudan University

Luke Qi Zhang is Associate Professor at the China Center for Economic Studies of the School of Economics at Fudan University. He specializes in the political economy of authoritarianism generally and how elite politics affects policy making and economic outcomes in China specifically. His book (co-authored with Mingxing Liu) *Revolutionary Legacy, Power Structure, and Grassroots Capitalism under the Red Flag in China* (Cambridge University Press, 2019) proposes a theory of localized property rights protection under authoritarianism, and applies the theory to the private sector development in both the Mao era and the current reform era in China.

Mingxing Liu

Peking University

Mingxing Liu is Professor of the China Institute for Educational Finance Research at Peking University. He works on China's elite politics, economic growth, and local governance. He has published numerous academic articles in international and Chinese journals such as the *American Political Science Review, Comparative Political Studies, Comparative Politics,* and *Journal of Politics.*

Daniel Mattingly

Yale University

Daniel Mattingly is Associate Professor in the Department of Political Science at Yale University. He studies the domestic and international politics of authoritarian regimes, with a focus on China. His book *The Art of Political Control in China* (Cambridge University Press, 2020) received the Best Book Award from the Democracy and Autocracy Section of the American Political Science Association and was named a best book of the year by *Foreign Affairs.*

Editorial Advisory Board

About the Series

The works in this Elements series examine China's economy, governance, and policy-making process. Members of the political and business communities will find the series a valuable guide to navigate China's complex policy and governance system and understand its business environment.

Cambridge Elements

Chinese Economy and Governance

Elements in the Series

Meritocracy or Patronage? Political Foundations of China's Economic Transition
Fubing Su and Ran Tao

Elite Conflicts and the Path to Economic Decentralization
Dong Zhang, Mingxing Liu and Victor Shih

Taxation and Governance in Contemporary China
Xiaobo Lü and Changdong Zhang

Bribery as a Third Path to Power? Political Selection in China Beyond Performanceand Patronage
Jiangnan Zhu

A full series listing is available at: www.cambridge.org/ECEG

Printed in the United Kingdom by TJ Clays Ltd.